Using the
Data Warehouse

Using the Data Warehouse

W.H. Inmon

R.D. Hackathorn

A Wiley–QED Publication

John Wiley & Sons, Inc.

New York • Chichester • Brisbane • Toronto • Singapore

Library of Congress Cataloging-in-Publication Data:

ISBN 0471-05966-8

Printed in the United States of America
10 9 8 7 6 5 4 3 2

This book is dedicated to Hung Le, the world's best System Developer.

Thân tăng ông Hùng Lê, một người System Developer giỏi nhất thế giới

Contents

Preface

From the conceptual origins of the single database serving all purposes has evolved the notion of a data architecture where data is divided into a data warehouse and an operational database. The evolution toward the architecture featuring a data warehouse is in response to many technological, economic, and organizational factors working symbiotically, simultaneously, and spontaneously: the difference in the users of the two environments, the difference in the technology supporting the two environments, the difference in the amount of data found in the two environments, the difference between the business usage of the two environments, and so forth.

The primary audience served by the data warehouse is one that can be called the DSS (decision support systems) community—the community making high-level and long-term managerial decisions. The data warehouse provides the foundation needed for effective DSS processing. It is true that DSS processing can be done without a data warehouse; but *effective* DSS processing cannot be done without one.

The data warehouse serves the EIS (executive information systems) community, the spreadsheet analysis community, the ad hoc reporting community, the periodic reporting community, and many others. There is a wide diversity in the uses for the data found in the data warehouse. The data in the data warehouse has essentially two characteristics—it is integrated and it is historic. Its integrated nature provides a foundation for doing corporatewide analysis; its historic nature provides a foundation for doing trend analysis and for looking at the corporation over the spectrum of time.

The data warehouse contains both detailed and summary data. The summary data serves the needs of top management in looking across broad vistas that are of interest to the corporation. The detailed data helps middle management to look at the more tactical aspects of the corporation; it also serves as a basis for future unknown investigations.

Metadata is another important part of the data warehouse environment. Metadata in the data warehouse is distinctly different from metadata found elsewhere in the data processing environment in both content and importance. Metadata in the data warehouse environment allows the DSS analyst serving at the pleasure of management to be proactive in the execution of his or her job.

People in the industry are no longer merely thinking about the data warehouse; they are now involved in its full-scale construction and deployment. The history of data warehouse has been documented in many books published by QED. The seminal reference is *Data Architecture: The Information Paradigm*. Herein is found the genesis of the notion of the data warehouse; the terms "data warehouse" and "information warehouse" were first used here. *Data Architecture* raised as many questions as were answered. One question that was raised was what the data warehouse looks like in terms of a specific technology. The description of data warehouse in terms of specific technologies was provided in books written for DB2, ORACLE, DEC's rDB, and TERADATA.

Following the books on data warehouse in specific technologies was the definitive book on its development, *Building the Data Warehouse,* aimed at the designer and developer who needed to come to grips with the issues of actually building the data warehouse. Many aspects of the data warehouse were described in the book, as well as a formal definition of what a data warehouse is, and design considerations.

This book—*Using the Data Warehouse*—is for the user and administrator of the data warehouse. Very little material will be presented on how to design or develop a data warehouse. Instead, it is assumed that the data warehouse is built (or is being built) and that the audience is the user who will be expected to make the most of it. In addition, there is some material for the administrator of the mature (or maturing) data warehouse environment.

Using the Data Warehouse, then, is an extension of the books that precede it. It is assumed that if there are questions as to practices, procedures, and philosophies, the reader can refer back to one or another of the preceding books.

This book is for anyone interested in data warehouse. Database administrators, data architects, data administrators, end-user liaisons, and managers of the data warehouse environment will all find the book invaluable.

The authors are indebted to the many people—coworkers, clients, friends, seminar attendees, and competitors—who shape the day-to-day experiences and observations of the author. Particular thanks go to:

Jim Ashbrook—PRISM Solutions
Arnie Barnett—Barnett Data Systems
Cheryl Estep—Chevron
Jeanne Friedman—independent consultant
Claudia Imhoff—independent consultant
Jim Kerr—Kerr Systems International
Hung Le—PRISM Solutions

Rick Patch—Sybase/MDI
Sue Osterfelt—Storage Tek
Judy Rawls—PRISM Solutions
Cynthia Schmidt—PRISM Solutions
Mike Schmidt—PRISM Solutions
Cass Squire—PRISM Solutions
J.D. Welch—PRISM Solutions
Ed Young—PRISM Solutions
John Zachman—independent consultant

WHI/RDH

Using the
Data Warehouse

The Data Warehouse

The starting point for the effective usage of the data warehouse is an understanding of what a data warehouse is. It has a very predictable shape and structure. The user of the data warehouse needs to know what the features and components of the data warehouse are before a serious discussion of its usage can ensue.

The data warehouse is the focal point of the architecture for information processing for modern computer systems. The data warehouse supports informational (i.e., DSS—decision support) processing by providing a solid foundation of integrated, corporatewide historical data from which to do management analysis. The data warehouse provides the basis for corporate integration in a world of older unintegrated application systems. Data warehouse is built and deployed in an evolutionary, step-by-step fashion. The data warehouse organizes and stores the data needed for informational, analytical processing over a long time perspective. From the historical foundation of data, trend analysis and slicing and dicing can be accomplished. There is indeed a world of promise in the support of the managerial function of the corporation in the construction and maintenance of a data warehouse. What, then, is a data warehouse?

DATA WAREHOUSE—A DEFINITION

A data warehouse is a

- subject-oriented,
- integrated,
- time-variant,
- nonvolatile

collection of data in support of management's decision-making process, as shown in Figure 1.1.

Raw elements of data entering the data warehouse come from the unintegrated operational environment (the older "legacy" systems environment) in almost every case. The data warehouse is always a store of data that is physically separated from the older operational, legacy systems environment even though the data in the warehouse is transformed from the application data found in the operational environment.

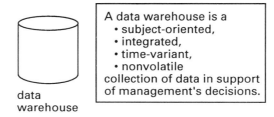

data
warehouse

A data warehouse is a
• subject-oriented,
• integrated,
• time-variant,
• nonvolatile
collection of data in support
of management's decisions.

Figure 1.1.   Data warehouse definition.

This academic definition of what a data warehouse is deserves a full explanation because there are some important features and subtleties underlying it.

SUBJECT ORIENTATION

The first notable characteristic of the data warehouse is that it is organized around the major subjects of the enterprise (i.e., the high-level entities of the enterprise). The orientation around the major subject areas of the corporation causes the data warehouse design to be "data driven." The data-driven subject organization of the data warehouse is in contrast to the more classical process/functional organization of applications, which characterize most older operational systems. Figure 1.2 shows the contrast between the two types of orientations.

The operational world is designed around applications and functions such as loans, savings, bank cards, and trust processing (in the case of a financial institution). The data warehouse world is organized around major subjects such as customer, vendor, product, and activity. The alignment of the data warehouse around major subject areas of the corporation affects the design and implementation of the data found in the data warehouse. Most prominently, the major subject area influences the key structure of the data and the organization of non-key data around those keys.

The application/functional world is concerned both with database design and process design. In truth, functional boundaries are the major criteria for the application designer. On the other hand, the data warehouse developer focuses on data modeling and database design exclusively. Process/functional design (in its classical form) is not part of the data warehouse development process.

The differences between process/function orientation of applications and subject/data-driven orientation of the data

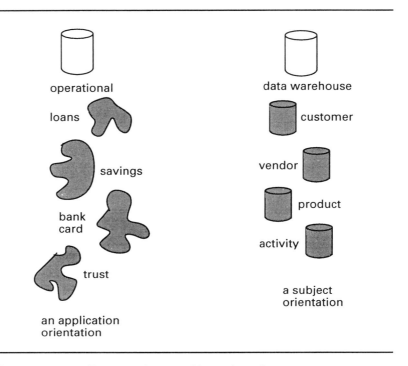

Figure 1.2.   Data warehouse subject orientation.

warehouse show up in the content of data. Data warehouse data does not include data that will not be used for DSS processing, while operational application-oriented data contains detailed data that satisfies immediate functional/processing requirements that may or may not have any relevance or interest to the DSS analyst.

Another important distinction between application-oriented operational data and data-driven warehouse data is apparent in the relationships of data. Operational application data relates to the immediate needs and concerns of the business—what is accurate and relevant right now. A relationship found in the operational environment is based on a current business rule that governs the ongoing relationship between two or more tables or databases. On the other hand, data warehouse data spans a spectrum of time and the data relationships between two or more tables may be many. Many business rules (and correspondingly, many data relationships) may be represented in the data warehouse between two or more tables. (For a detailed explanation of how data relationships are managed in the data warehouse, refer to the Tech Topic published by Prism Solutions on data relationships.)

From the perspective of the fundamental difference between a functional/process application orientation and a subject orientation, there is a major difference between operational systems and data and the data warehouse.

INTEGRATION

Easily the most important feature of the data warehouse environment and its second distinctive characteristic, is that data housed within it is integrated. With integration, the data warehouse takes on a very corporate flavor.

The integration of data warehouse data shows up in many different ways—in consistent naming conventions, consistent measurement of variables, consistent encoding structures, consistent physical attributes of data, and so forth.

Contrast the integration found within the data warehouse with the lack of integration found in the applications environment, and the differences are stark, as shown by Figure 1.3.

Over the years, many applications designers have made their individual decisions as to how an application should be built. The style and the customized design decisions of the application designer show up in a hundred ways such as in

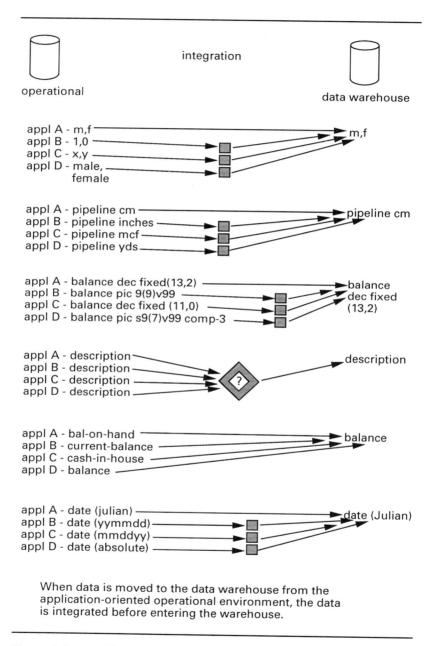

When data is moved to the data warehouse from the application-oriented operational environment, the data is integrated before entering the warehouse.

Figure 1.3. Data integration.

differences in encoding, differences in key structures, differences in physical characteristics, differences in naming conventions, and so forth. The collective ability of many application designers to create inconsistent applications is legendary.

Figure 1.3 shows some of the most important differences in the ways applications are designed:

- *encoding*—Application designers have chosen to encode the field, gender, in different ways. One designer represents gender as an "m" and an "f". Another application designer represents gender as a "1" and a "0". Another application designer represents gender as an "x" and a "y". Yet another application designer represents gender as "male" and "female." It doesn't matter much how gender arrives in the data warehouse. "M" and "F" are probably as good as any representation. What matters is that whatever source gender comes from, that gender arrives in the data warehouse in a consistent integrated state. Therefore, when gender is loaded into the data warehouse from an application where it has been represented in other than an "M" and "F" format, the data must be converted to the single, consistent data warehouse format.
- *measurement of attributes*—Application designers have chosen to measure pipeline in a variety of ways over the years. One designer stores pipeline data in centimeters. Another stores pipeline data in terms of inches. Another stores pipeline data in units of millions of cubic feet per second. And another designer stores pipeline information in terms of yards. Whatever the application source, when the pipeline information arrives in the data warehouse it needs to be measured the same way.

As shown in Figure 1.3, the issues of integration affect almost every aspect of design—the physical characteristics of data, the dilemma of having more than one source of data, and the issues of inconsistent naming standards, inconsistent date formats, and so forth.

Whatever the design issue, the result is the same: The data needs to be stored in the data warehouse in a single, globally acceptable fashion even when the underlying operational application systems store the data differently.

When the DSS analyst approaches the data warehouse, the focus of the analyst should be on using the data that is in the warehouse, rather than on wondering about the credibility or consistency of the data.

TIME VARIANCY

All data in the data warehouse is accurate as of some moment in time. This basic characteristic of data in the warehouse is very different from that of data found in the operational environment. In the operational environment, data is accurate as of the moment of access. In other words, in the operational environment, when you access a unit of data, you expect that it will reflect accurate values as of the moment of access. This is the third defining feature of the data warehouse.

Because data in the data warehouse is accurate as of some moment in time (i.e., not "right now"), data found in the warehouse is said to be "time variant." Figure 1.4 shows the time variancy of data warehouse data.

The time variancy of data warehouse data shows up in several ways. The simplest way is that data warehouse data represents data over a long time horizon—from five to ten years. The time horizon represented for the operational environment is much shorter—from the current values of today up to sixty to ninety days. Applications that must perform well and must be available for transaction processing must carry the minimum amount of data if they are to

operational

current value data:
- time horizon—60–90 days
- key may or may not have an element of time
- data can be updated

data warehouse

snapshot data:
- time horizon—5–10 years
- key contains an element of time
- once snapshot is made, record cannot be updated

Figure 1.4.   Time variancy.

have any degree of flexibility at all. Therefore, operational applications have a short time horizon, as a matter of sound application design.

The key structure is the second way that time variancy shows up in the data warehouse. Every key structure in the data warehouse contains, implicitly or explicitly, an element of time, such as day, week, and month. The element of time is almost always at the bottom of the concatenated key found in the data warehouse. On occasions, the element of time will exist implicitly, such as the case where an entire file is duplicated at the end of the month, or the quarter.

The third way that time variancy appears is that data warehouse data, once correctly recorded, cannot be updated. Data warehouse data is, for all practical purposes, a long series of snapshots. Of course, if the snapshot has been taken incorrectly, then it can be corrected. But assuming that snapshots are made properly, they are not altered once made. In some cases it may be unethical or even illegal for the snapshots in the data warehouse to be altered. Operational data, being accurate as of the moment of access, can be updated as the need arises.

NONVOLATILITY

The fourth defining characteristic of the data warehouse is that it is nonvolatile. Figure 1.5 illustrates this aspect of the data warehouse, showing that updates—inserts, deletes, and changes—are regularly done to the operational environment on a record-by-record basis. But the basic manipulation of data that occurs in the data warehouse is much simpler. There are only two kinds of operations that occur in the data warehouse: the initial loading of data, and the access of data. There is no update of data (in the general sense of *update*) in the data warehouse as a normal part of processing.

There are some very powerful consequences of this basic difference between operational processing and data warehouse processing. At the design level, the need to be cautious of the update anomaly is no factor in the data warehouse, since update of data is not done. This means that at the physical level of design, liberties can be taken to optimize

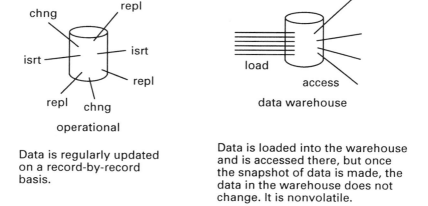

chng
repl
isrt
isrt
repl
repl
chng

operational

Data is regularly updated on a record-by-record basis.

load
access
data warehouse

Data is loaded into the warehouse and is accessed there, but once the snapshot of data is made, the data in the warehouse does not change. It is nonvolatile.

Figure 1.5.   Dynamic versus static data.

the access of data, particularly in dealing with the issues of normalization and physical denormalization. Another consequence of the simplicity of data warehouse operation is in the underlying technology used to run the data warehouse environment. Having to support record-by-record update in an online mode (as is often the case with operational processing) requires technology that has a very complex foundation underneath a façade of simplicity. The technology supporting backup and recovery, transaction and data integrity, and the detection and remedy of deadlock is quite complex and unnecessary for data warehouse processing.

The definitive characteristics of a data warehouse—subject orientation of design, integration of data within the data warehouse, time variancy, and simplicity of data management—all lead to an environment that is *very* different from the classical operational applications environment.

The source of nearly all data warehouse data is the operational environment. It is a temptation to think that there is massive redundancy of data between the operational and the data warehouse environment; indeed, that is the first impression many people have. But in fact there is little or no redundancy between the two environments and claiming that there is demonstrates a lack of understanding as to what is occurring in the data warehouse.

Consider the following:

- Data is filtered as it passes from the operational environment to the data warehouse environment. Much data never passes out of the operational environment. Only data that is needed for DSS processing finds its way into the data warehouse environment.
- The time horizon of data is very different from one environment to the next. Data in the operational environment is very fresh. Data in the warehouse is much older.

From the perspective of time horizons alone, there is very little overlap between the operational and the data warehouse environments.

- The data warehouse contains summary data that is never found in the operational environment.
- Data undergoes a fundamental transformation as it passes into the data warehouse. Figure 1.3 illustrates that most data is significantly altered upon being selected for and moving into the data warehouse. Said another way, most data is physically and radically altered as it moves into the warehouse. It is not the same data that resides in the operational environment from the standpoint of integration.

In light of these factors, data redundancy between the two environments is a rare occurrence, resulting in less than 1 percent redundancy between the two environments.

THE STRUCTURE OF THE WAREHOUSE

The data warehouse has a distinct structure. There are different levels of summarization and detail that demark the data warehouse. In addition, there are different levels of age of data in the data warehouse. The general structure of a data warehouse is shown in Figure 1.6.

The different components of the data warehouse are:

- current detail data,
- old detail data,
- lightly summarized data,
- highly summarized data, and
- metadata.

There are several reasons why the major area of concern is the current detail data.

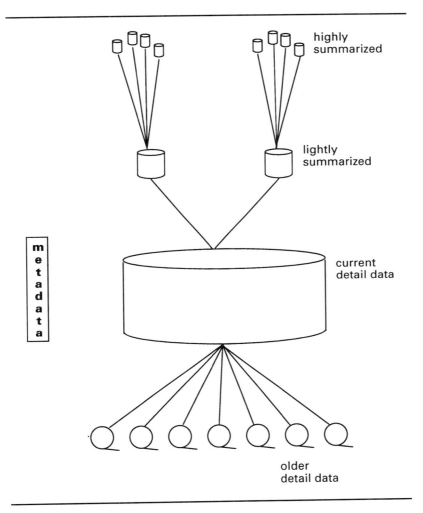

Figure 1.6.   The structure of data inside the data warehouse.

- Current detail data reflects the most recent happenings, which are always of great interest.
- Current detail data is voluminous because it is stored at the lowest level of granularity.

- Current detail data is almost always stored on disk storage, which is fast to access but expensive and complex to manage.

Older detail data is data that is stored on some form of mass storage. It is infrequently accessed and is stored at a level of detail consistent with current detailed data. While it is not mandatory that it be stored on an alternate medium, because of the anticipated large volume of data coupled with the infrequent access of the data, the storage medium for older detail data is usually not on disk.

Lightly summarized data is data that is distilled from the low level of detail found at the current detailed level. This level of the data warehouse is almost always stored on disk. The design issues facing the data architect in building this level of the data warehouse are the following:

- Over what unit of time is the summarization done?
- What contents—attributes—will the lightly summarized data contain?

The next level of data found in the data warehouse is that of the highly summarized data. Highly summarized data is compact and easily accessible. Sometimes this data is found in the data warehouse environment and in other cases it is found outside the immediate walls of the technology that houses the data warehouse. (In any case, the highly summarized data is part of the data warehouse regardless of where the data is physically housed.)

The final component of the data warehouse is that of metadata. In many ways metadata sits in a different dimension than other data warehouse data, because metadata contains no data directly taken from the operational environment. Metadata plays a special and very important role in the data warehouse, and is used in various ways:

- It is a directory to help the DSS analyst locate the contents of the data warehouse.
- It is a guide to the mapping of data as the data is transformed from the operational environment to the data warehouse environment.
- It is a guide to the algorithms used for summarization between the current detail data and the lightly summarized data and the lightly summarized data and the highly summarized data, etc.

Metadata plays a much more important role in the data warehouse environment than it ever did in the classical operational environment.

In order to bring to life the different levels of data found in the data warehouse, consider the example shown in Figure 1.7. In the figure, old sales detail is that detail about sales that is older than 1991. All sales detail from 1982 (or whenever the data architect is able to start collecting archival detail) is stored in the old detail level of data.

The current value detail contains data from 1991 to 1994 (assuming that 1994 is the current year). As a rule, sales detail does not find its way into the current level of detail until at least twenty-four hours have passed since the sales information became available to the operational environment. In other words, there was a time lag of at least twenty-four hours between the time the operational environment got news of the sale and the moment the sales data was entered into the data warehouse.

The sales detail is summarized weekly by subproduct line and by region to produce the lightly summarized stores of data.

The weekly sales detail is further summarized monthly along even broader lines to produce the highly summarized data.

Metadata contains at least the following information:

- the structure of the data
- the algorithms used for summarization
- the mapping from the operational to the data warehouse

Note that not every summarization ever done gets stored in the data warehouse. There will be many occasions where analysis will be done and one type of summary or another

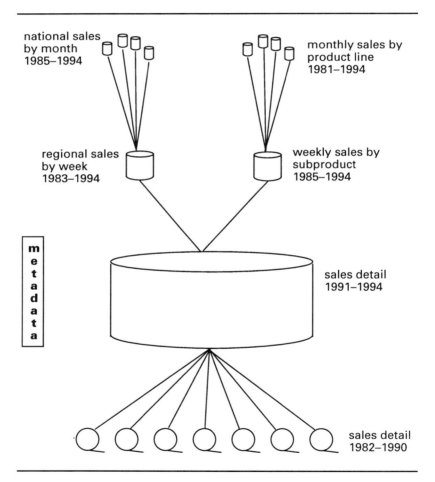

national sales by month 1985–1994

monthly sales by product line 1981–1994

regional sales by week 1983–1994

weekly sales by subproduct 1985–1994

metadata

sales detail 1991–1994

sales detail 1982–1990

Figure 1.7. Levels of summarization that might be found in the data warehouse.

will be produced. The only type of summarization that is permanently stored in the data warehouse is that of summary data that is frequently used. In other words, if a DSS analyst produces a summarized result that has a very low probability of ever being used again, then that summarization is not stored in the data warehouse.

OLD DETAIL STORAGE MEDIUM

The symbol shown in Figure 1.7 for old detail storage medium is that of magnetic tape. Indeed, magnetic tape may be used to store that type of data in the data warehouse. In fact, Figure 1.8 shows a wide variety of storage media that should be considered for storing old detail data, depending on the volume of data, the frequency of access, the cost of the media, and the type of access.

FLOW OF DATA

There is a normal and predictable flow of data within the data warehouse, depicted in Figure 1.9. Data enters the data warehouse from the operational environment. (Note: There

> • photo-optical storage
> • RAID
> • microfiche
> • magnetic tape
> • mass storage

The storage medium for the bulk portion of the data warehouse can be a wide variety of storage types.

Figure 1.8.   Storage media.

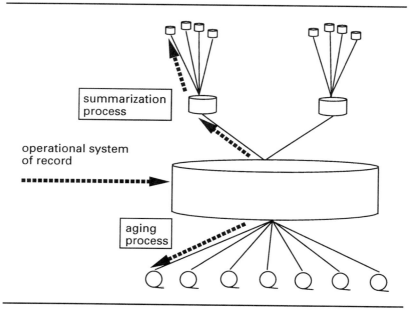

Figure 1.9. The flow of data inside the data warehouse.

are a few very interesting exceptions to this rule. However, *nearly all* data enters the data warehouse from the operational environment.) As data enters the data warehouse from the operational environment, it is transformed, as has been described earlier.

Upon entering the data warehouse, data goes into the current detail level of detail, as shown in the figure. It resides there and is used there until one of three events occurs:

- it is purged,
- it is summarized, and/or
- it is archived.

The aging process inside a data warehouse moves current detail data to old detail data, based on the age of data.

The summarization process uses the detail of data to calculate the lightly summarized data and the highly summarized levels of data.

USING THE DATA WAREHOUSE

Not surprisingly, the different levels of data within the data warehouse receive different levels of usage. As a rule, the higher the level of summarization, the more the data is used, as shown in Figure 1.10. Here we see that much usage oc-

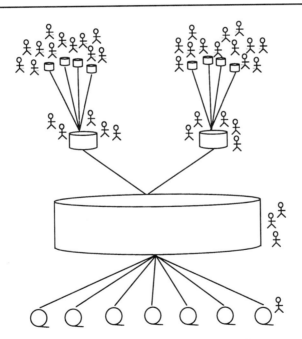

The higher the levels of summarization,
the more the usage of the data.

Figure 1.10.   Correlation of summarization levels to data usage.

curs in the highly summarized data, while the old detail data is hardly ever used.

There is a good reason for moving the organization to the paradigm suggested in Figure 1.10—*resource utilization.* The more summarized the data, the quicker and the more efficient it is to get to the data. If a shop finds that it is doing much processing at the detailed levels of the data warehouse, then a correspondingly large amount of machine resources are being consumed. It is in everyone's best interest to do processing at as high a level of summarization as possible.

For many shops, the DSS analyst in a pre–data warehouse environment has used data at the detailed level. In many ways, getting to detailed data is like having a security blanket, even when other levels of summarization are available. One of the tasks of the data architect is to wean the DSS user from constantly using data at the lowest level of detail. There are two motivators at the disposal of the data architect:

- installing a chargeback system, where the end user pays for resources consumed, and
- pointing out that very good response time can be achieved when dealing with data at a high level of summarization, while poor response time results from dealing with data at a low level of detail.

OTHER CONSIDERATIONS

There are some other considerations in building and administering the data warehouse, as shown in Figure 1.11. The first is that of indexes. Data at the higher levels of summarization can be freely indexed, while data at the lower levels of detail is so voluminous that it can be only indexed sparingly. By the same token, data at the high levels of detail can be restructured relatively easily, while the volume of

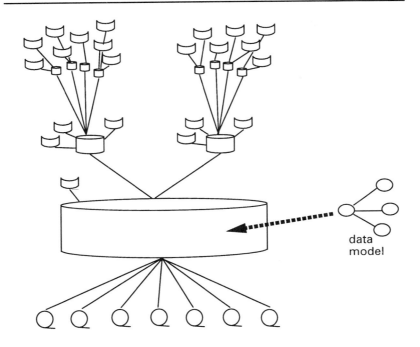

• The more summarized the data is, the more indices there are.
• The data model applies to the current level of detail.

Figure 1.11.   Summarized data and number of indices.

data at the lower levels is so great that data cannot be easily restructured.

Accordingly, the data model and formal design work done that lays the foundation for the data warehouse applies almost exclusively to the current level of detail. In other words, the data modeling activities do not apply to the levels of summarization, in almost every case.

Another structural consideration is that of the partitioning of data warehouse data. Figure 1.12 shows that current level detail is almost always partitioned. This partitioning

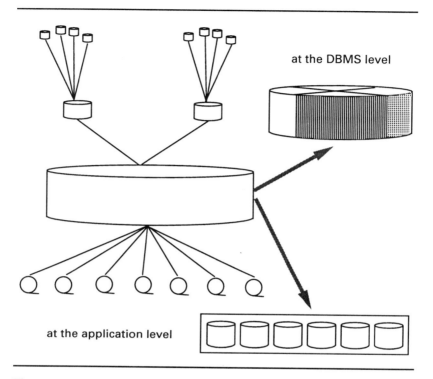

at the DBMS level

at the application level

Figure 1.12. Partitioned current detailed data.

can be done in two ways—at the DBMS (data base management system) level and at the application level. In DBMS partitioning, the DBMS is aware of the partitions and manages them accordingly. In the case of application partitioning, only the application programmer is aware of the partitions, and responsibility for the management of the partitions is left up to the programmer.

Under DBMS partitioning, much infrastructure work is done automatically. But there is a tremendous degree of inflexibility associated with the automatic management of the partitions. In the case of application partitioning of data warehouse data, much work falls to the programmer, but the end result is much flexibility in the management of data in the data warehouse.

AN EXAMPLE OF A DATA WAREHOUSE

Figure 1.13 shows a hypothetical example of a data warehouse structured for a manufacturing environment. The figure shows only current detail data. The levels of summarization are not shown, nor is the old detail archive shown. There are tables of the same type divided over time. For example, for parts manufacture history, there are many physically separate tables, each representing a different quarter. The structure of the data is consistent within the parts manufacture history table, even though there are physically many tables that logically comprise the history.

Note that for different types of tables there are different units of time physically dividing the units of data. Manufacturing history is divided by quarter, part/order history is divided by year, and customer history is a single file, not divided by time at all.

Also note that the different tables are linked by means of a common identifier—parts, parts/orders, and so on. (*Note:* The representation of a relationship in the data warehouse environment takes a very different form than relationships represented in other environments, such as the operational environment. Refer to the Tech Topic by Prism Solutions on data relationships in the data warehouse for an in-depth explanation.)

OTHER ANOMALIES

While the data warehouse components work in the fashion described for almost all data, there are a few worthwhile exceptions that need to be discussed. One exception is that

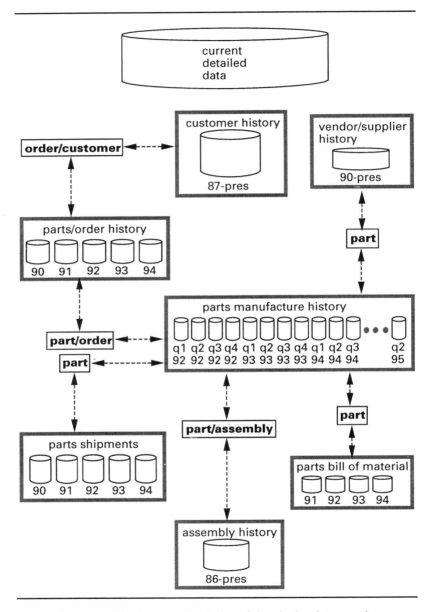

Figure 1.13. The internal structuring of data in the data warehouse.

of public summary data. Public summary data is summary data that has been calculated outside the boundaries of the data warehouse but is used throughout the corporation. Public summary data is stored and managed in the data warehouse, even though its calculation is well outside the data warehouse. A classical example of public summary data is the quarterly filings made by every public company to the SEC. The accountants work to produce such numbers as quarterly revenue, quarterly expenses, and quarterly profit. The work done by the accountants is well outside the data warehouse. However, those benchmark numbers produced by the accountants are used widely within the corporation— by marketing, sales, and so forth. Once the SEC filing is done, the data is stored in the data warehouse.

SUMMARY

A data warehouse is a subject-oriented, integrated, time-variant, nonvolatile collection of data in support of management's decision needs. Each of the salient aspects of a data warehouse carries its own implications.

In addition, there are four levels of data warehouse data:

- old detail,
- current detail,
- lightly summarized data, and
- highly summarized data.

Metadata is also an important part of the data warehouse environment. Each of the levels of detail carry their own considerations.

2

The Operational Data Store

The world of the data warehouse has opened up informational processing for the DSS analyst. With the data warehouse comes the possibility of using information for the corporation in a competitive fashion. But with informational processing comes a hybrid form of the data warehouse, called the *operational data store (ODS)*. The DSS analyst is able to do informational processing from either the data warehouse or its variant form, the ODS. However, there are some very real and important differences between the two environments. These differences are relevant to the DSS analyst because trying to do data warehouse informational-style processing on an ODS is asking for trouble, just as trying to do ODS-style informational processing on a data warehouse is asking for trouble. It therefore is important the DSS analyst understand what an ODS is, how it is different from a data warehouse, and what its appropriate usage is.

LIMITATIONS OF THE DATA WAREHOUSE

As important and strategic as the data warehouse is, the data warehouse does nothing for the corporation that is struggling with lack of integration in the operational environment (as opposed to the DSS environment). The data warehouse is strictly and only applicable to the DSS environment, not the operational environment. (For a much more in-depth discussion of the differences between these environments, refer to *Data Architecture: The Information Paradigm* QED/Wiley.)

Over the years most corporations have built a large and disorganized collection of older operational applications, affectionately called the "legacy systems" environment or the "spider web" environment. These older operational applications have served as the backbone of the day-to-day processing of the corporation for many years. These applications have been built from business requirements as they were understood a quarter-century ago. In most cases, these older operational applications have been patched to the point of being fragile. In short, the legacy systems environment is a difficult world to live and conduct business in today.

It is normal for the older operational application environment to be terribly unintegrated. After all, the applications were built one at a time, separately and distinctly from other applications. But recognizing the difficulties with older operational legacy applications is one thing—doing something about the lack of integration is something else.

A typical response of the IS (Information Systems) developer to the challenge posed by the lack of integration of older operational applications is to try to apply the techniques of information engineering or to build a data model and a process model that reflects the integrated informational needs of the corporation. Building the integrated data and process models of where the corporation needs to go is a good start to the achievement of integration. Unfortunately, as soon as it comes time to cast the integrated models into the mold of real systems, problems with implementation begin to surface. For many reasons, the translation of data models and process models into new systems starting from a base of older, unintegrated operational applications in a rational, affordable fashion is a very hard transition.

A broader assault on the challenge posed by older unintegrated operational applications is that of reengineering. While there is much promise to the technique of reengineering, achieving short-term, tangible, cost-effective results in the quest for operational integration remains elusive.

THE OPERATIONAL DATA STORE

Into this world of intransigent, unintegrated legacy applications comes the notion of the *operational data store (ODS)*. The ODS is the extension of the data warehouse into the world of operational systems. The ODS does not apply to informational processing outside the day-to-day operational arena. The ODS provides a foundation to achieve tangible integrated operational results in a reasonably short time frame. While the data warehouse offers no relief to the organization struggling with the operational aspects of unintegrated operational systems, the ODS offers immediate relief. Figure 2.1 shows the architecture in which the ODS resides. Here is a clear demarcation between the operational and DSS worlds. The ODS clearly is in the operational domain. Data enters the ODS from older unintegrated applications, just as it does in the data warehouse.

MIXING THE ODS AND THE DATA WAREHOUSE

When the ODS is first discovered, there is the temptation to try to mix the ODS with the data warehouse. The temptation is strong. However:

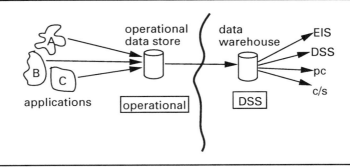

Figure 2.1. The architecture of which the operational data store is an integral part.

> In all cases, the ODS should be built separate and apart
> from the data warehouse. *There are no conditions under
> which the data warehouse and the ODS should ever be
> combined.*

There are many fundamental and important differences between the ODS and the data warehouse. The largest difference between the two environments lies in the content and structure of data found in the ODS and in the data warehouse. The ODS contains current-valued and near-current-valued data. The data warehouse contains historical data, as well as near-current-valued data. The ODS contains almost exclusively detail data while the data warehouse contains a rich supply of detail and summary data. The ODS is able to be updated while the data warehouse contains records that are snapshots. Figure 2.2 shows the difference between the ODS and the data warehouse.

In addition, there is some amount of operational data that will never be used for DSS processing that never makes its way into the data warehouse.

Although the diagram in Figure 2.2 shows the major dif-

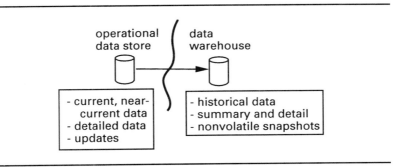

Figure 2.2.   Major differences between the two environments.

ferences between the ODS and the data warehouse, the dramatic differences between the populations of data are not evident. In general, there is much more data in the data warehouse than there is in the ODS. Figure 2.3 shows the proportionate difference between the volume of data found in the two environments.

In the same vein, the differences in the types of data contained within the two environments can be typified as the difference between homogeneity and heterogeneity. Figure 2.4 shows that the ODS contains homogeneous current-valued data while the data warehouse contains a vast supply of very heterogeneous data.

Another major difference between the ODS and the data

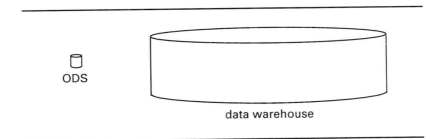

Figure 2.3.   The two environments drawn to scale.

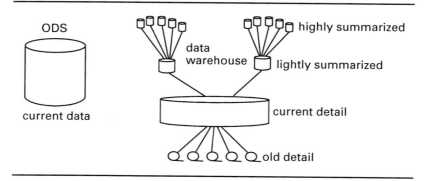

Figure 2.4.   The variety of data in a data warehouse.

warehouse lies not in the data contained in the warehouse, but in the underlying technology needed to support the two environments. The ODS requires a full-function, update-, record-oriented environment. The data warehouse, on the other hand, requires a simpler load-and-access technology. The major differences between the two technologies are shown in Figure 2.5.

In addition to the very real differences between the two environments in terms of data and technology, there is the difference in terms of the audience. The ODS serves a clerical or corporate day-to-day decision-making audience. The data warehouse serves the DSS analyst or management-oriented community. The ODS is used for up-to-the-second decisions. The data warehouse is used for long-term analysis and trend detection.

SUMMARY DATA IN THE ODS

Although the ODS contains primarily detailed data, there may be some small amounts of summary data in the ODS. The summary data is usually difficult to keep current and accurate so there is not very much of it. But in terms of

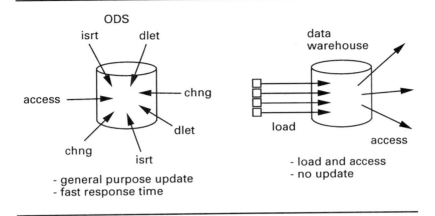

Figure 2.5.   The differences in the technologies of the two environments.

giving management a snapshot perspective of key corporate variables, the ODS can contain useful summary information. ODS summary data is used for inventory management, reservations management, retail sales management, and so

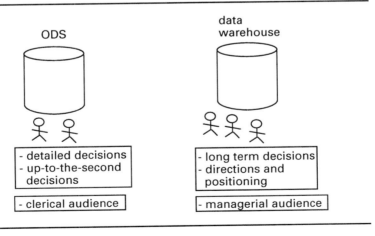

Figure 2.6.   The differences in audience.

forth. It is understood that ODS summary data is accurate only as of the moment it is accessed. Given that ODS data can be updated, a figure that is quoted as of 10:02 A.M. based on ODS data may well be inaccurate as of 10:03 A.M.

This important distinction between the ODS and the data warehouse shows up in several ways. For example, the summary data in the ODS is not able to be reconstructed (under any normal set of circumstances). In the data warehouse reports are able to be recreated if necessary down to the penny by carefully reconstructing the time period for which the report was written. But in the ODS, such a reconstruction is not possible. Nevertheless there can be great use for current summary data even if it cannot be reconstructed.

DEFINING THE ODS

What exactly is an ODS? As depicted in Figure 2.7, an ODS is a

- subject-oriented,
- integrated,
- volatile (i.e., able to be updated),

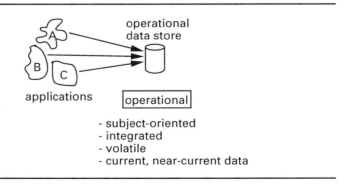

Figure 2.7.   The definition of an ODS.

- current or near-current collection of data in support of day-to-day detailed operational decisions.

The ODS is used almost exclusively for the operational information processing of the corporation.

The ODS is different from the data warehouse in the last two points—the data warehouse is nonvolatile while the ODS is volatile, and the data warehouse contains a long history of data while the ODS contains current and near-current data.

There is a transformation of data required to place data in the ODS as it passes out of the older applications in which it is initially housed. The transformation of data removes the application flavor of data and recreates the data in a corporate mold. The transformation includes activities such as the following:

- converting data
- deciding which data of multiple sources is the best
- summarizing data
- decoding/encoding data
- altering key structures
- altering physical structures
- reformatting data
- internally rerepresenting data
- recalculating data

SOME EXAMPLES

The easiest way to illustrate what an ODS looks like is through some examples. The first example is of very stable data, such as customer data. Figure 2.8 shows an ODS created out of several older applications.

The ODS contains data that is an amalgamation of the data that exists for a customer over multiple accounts. In

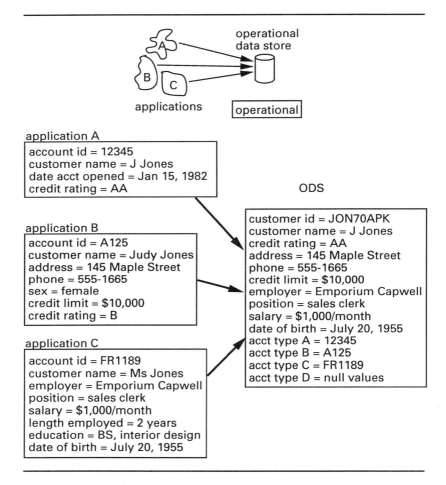

Figure 2.8. Creating the integrated record from the various
applications.

some cases, data in the ODS has several application sources,
and logic is needed to be able to determine what the best
source of data is. In other cases, there is only one source of
data in the application environment. When this is the case,
a default value is needed in the eventuality that there is no
application source for a given customer. Sometimes, data

exists in the application environment when there is no ODS data. This data is not needed for ODS processing.

One of the features of the ODS is the creation of a common key so that data can come from multiple sources and arrive at the appropriate ODS record. In addition, a reference in the ODS exists back to the application source, referring to the key value in the application, so that there is no confusion as to the linkage between records.

In Figure 2.8, there is a fourth type of account—account type D—that has no entry for the ODS customer record. One of the characteristics of this type of data in the ODS is that the data is not changed frequently. Only upon a change in the customer data will an update to the ODS be generated.

But not all data is stable and of a relatively low volume. Some data, typically transaction data, is of a very high volume. The ODS is able to manage this style of data, but in a different manner from that shown in Figure 2.8.

Figure 2.9 is an example of how high-volume data may be handled in an ODS. Here, we see that one technique for handling transaction data in the ODS is to aggregate data (i.e., create a profile of data) over some period of time, such as a week. The weekly transactions are gathered (or are otherwise calculated) and are placed into a record in the ODS.

Of course, when the aggregation is at such a high level that the informational needs of the organization are not being met, then a lower level of detail is needed in the ODS. The ultimate way of storing transaction data in the ODS is simply to store the transactions themselves. While such storage can be done (and is shown in the example in the bottom of Figure 2.9) there is an extremely high cost in storage and processing time. Raising the level of granularity of data is almost always the best bet for the building of the ODS when it comes to the management of transaction data. Only where there is a small amount of transaction data (an oxymoron!) can the raw storage of transactions be considered in the ODS.

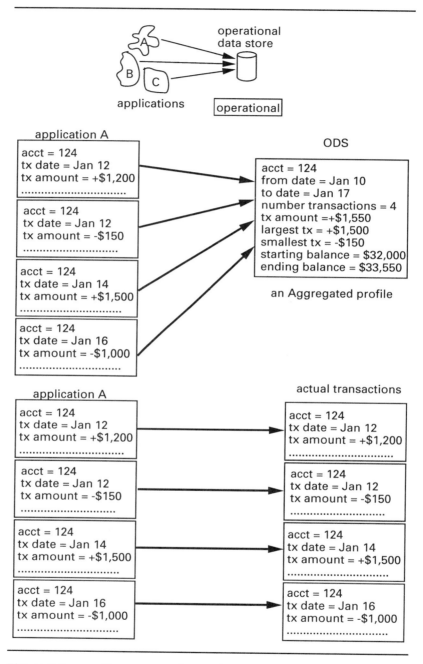

Figure 2.9.   Two common forms of transaction data in an ODS.

THE SYSTEM OF RECORD

An essential part of the ODS environment is the definition of the system of record. The system of record is the application data that feeds the ODS. The system of record is made up of the "best" older application data that should be used by the corporation. The "best" data in the older application environment is that which is the most

- timely,
- accurate,
- complete,
- structurally compatible with the data model, and
- nearest to the originating source.

Figure 2.10 shows the system of record.

The system of record requires a formal definition. The source of ODS data for a given element of data may be from a single file or data-base or from multiple files and data-bases. The underlying technologies of the older application systems do not have to be compatible with the ODS, or even

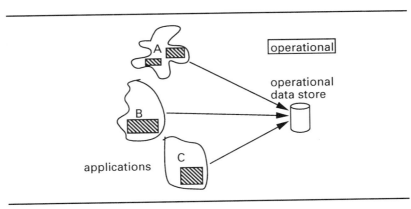

Figure 2.10.   The system of record—the essential part of the ODS.

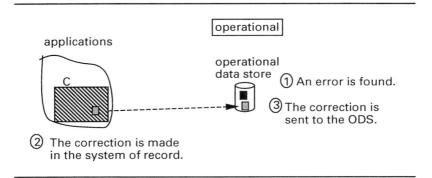

Figure 2.11.   The mechanics of update.

with the underlying technology found in other older application systems. The only technological requirement is that
data be passed efficiently from the older application environment to the technological environment supporting the
ODS.

Once the identification of the system of record is made,
the population of the ODS can commence. The population is
usually straightforward. However, when it becomes necessary to update data in the ODS either because the data is
incorrect or because the data in the ODS is out of date, the
change to the data must first be made in the system of record.
Figure 2.11 illustrates making changes to data in the system of record.

After the data is updated in the system of record, it is
then passed to the ODS, as shown in the figure. It is patently incorrect to update the ODS without first changing
the data in the system of record.

There are several styles of update that can occur in the
ODS:

- simple insertion of data,
- the insert/replace of data,

- the field replacement of data,
- field accumulation of data, and
- accumulation of records of data.

Fig 2.12 shows the typical techniques of refreshment of data.

The *simple insertion* of data requires that when a record is created in the older application environment, that the same record be inserted into the ODS. In this case, it is possible to generate multiple records for the same key in the ODS. If multiple records of the same type for the same key is what is desired, then simple insertion is the appropriate technique.

The technique of *insert/replace* is the same as simple insertion except that when a record is to be inserted into the ODS, the inserting program checks to see if a record with the same key already exists in the ODS. If a record does exist, then a replacement is made, rather than an insertion. In this way no records with duplicate keys can be created in the ODS.

The third technique on our list is that of the *field replace*.

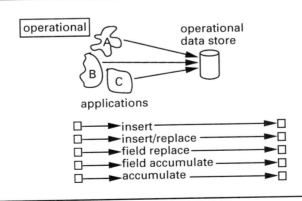

Figure 2.12.   The types of inserts/updates into the ODS.

The field replace requires that when a record is created in the older application environment the field(s) identified in the older environment be replaced into a field of the same type in the ODS for the same key. If a record in the ODS is not found upon the occasion of replacement, then a new record is created in the ODS. Default values are supplied in the ODS for the fields not provided by the older application environment.

The fourth technique is that of *field accumulation*. This applies only to numeric fields and is the same as field replace except that individual fields are accumulated instead of replaced.

The last technique is that of *accumulation of records*. In this case, multiple records from the older application environment are accumulated to form a record in the ODS.

There are many combinations and permutations of these basic approaches to the loading of data into the ODS.

Another dimension of the loading process is that of the lapse between the time of change in the operational application and the time when the change is reflected in the ODS. As a rule, the application environment updates the ODS every two to four hours, although there may be significant variations in this. Figure 2.13 shows the time lag between the update of the operational environment and the ensuing update in the ODS.

There are several issues relating to the lengthening or the shortening of this time lag. As a rule, the more you shrink it, the more you incur complexity and expense. Trying to go from a one-hour time lag to a ten-minute time lag is a very expensive proposition and entails the use of technology other than that found in the mainstream. On the other hand, trying to go to a 12-hour time lag may decrease costs and complexity, but may diminish the usefulness of the data in the ODS.

Because of the volume of data found in the transaction processing environment, because of the potential performance

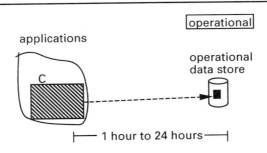

Figure 2.13.   A typical time lag between refreshments.

interruption of loading transaction data into the ODS, and because of the potential volume of data found in the online, high-performance transaction environment, there is a questionable fit between the ODS and the online high-performance transaction environment. Figure 2.14 illustrates this uneasy fit. Of course, the two environments can be married together. However, careful consideration needs to be given to the technology, the business justification, and the design of the marriage.

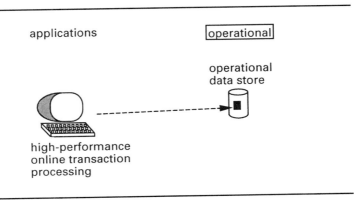

Figure 2.14.   A somewhat uncomfortable fit.

TRAPPING DELTA DATA

The data that flows into the ODS from the older application environment is often called *delta data*. Delta data is data that changes—is updated, inserted, or deleted—in the older application environment that needs to be reflected in the ODS. There are several ways to trap delta data in the operational applications. Figure 2.15 shows the common ways of trapping delta data.

Delta data is trapped most simply at the application level. The applications running the operational environment sense that a change has occurred and write a record off to the ODS. A second way that delta data is trapped is in the creation of a delta file. In this case the delta data is written off to a delta file that is later processed by the ODS. A third way is at the DBMS level. The DBMS senses that a change is being made to the database and writes the "after" image record off to the delta data file. Later the delta data file is processed against the ODS.

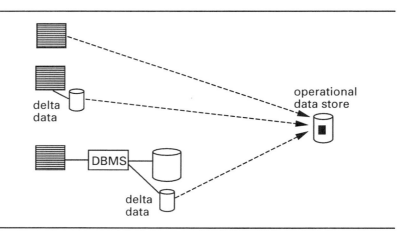

Figure 2.15.   The common ways of trapping data for refreshment into the ODS.

COLLAPSING APPLICATION DATA UPON ENTRY IN THE ODS

A standard design technique for the management of large amounts of data is that of "collapsing" the volumes of data upon entry into the ODS. Figure 2.16 depicts the technique.

One way of collapsing data—that of aggregating it—has already been discussed. But there are other ways in which data is collapsed, such as summarization, the use of rolling summary structures, the use of selective indexes to point to detailed entries, the use of selective samples, the use of selective subsets of data, and so forth. In every case, the benefit is that the ODS is not drowned in a large volume of data. The limited volume of data that enters the ODS is much more manageable—able to be reorganized, indexed, scanned, and restructured. (This design topic is commonly known as *raising the granularity of data.*)

There is, however, a tradeoff that is made. Whenever data is collapsed—*however it is collapsed*—some amount of functionality is lost. The tradeoff, functionality for manageability when made judiciously, can be a very beneficial feature of the architecture.

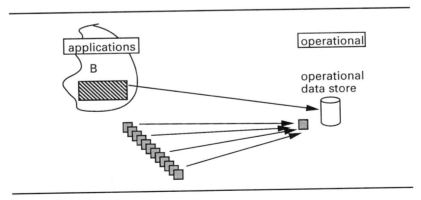

Figure 2.16.   Collapsing application data.

MOVING THE SYSTEM OF RECORD TO THE ODS

After the ODS is initially built, it is natural to ask the question "Can we build the system of record in the ODS?" Figure 2.17 shows the election to build part of the system of record in the ODS.

Of course, some or all of the system of record may be built inside the ODS. There is no technological reason why such a design cannot be conceived. There are, however, many potential difficulties that must be considered in shifting the system of record to the ODS. In general, the ODS should not contain the system of record unless there are extenuating circumstances.

The first design consideration is whether all of the system of record should be shifted to the ODS. In almost every case, only part of the system of record should be shifted. Figure 2.18 shows the shifting of part of the system of record to the ODS.

Attempting to shift *all* of the system of record to the ODS, and certainly all of the system of record all at once, is a gargantuan task requiring much development effort and entail-

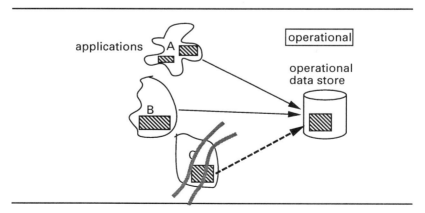

Figure 2.17. Moving the system of record to the ODS—considerations.

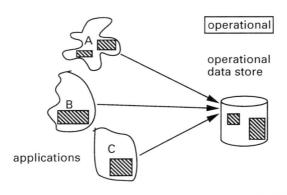

operational

operational
data store

applications

Figure 2.18.   Data stored in legacy systems and the ODS.

ing much risk. Normally it doesn't make sense to attempt to shift all of the system of record in a single move. If the system of record is to be moved to the ODS, it should be moved one component (or one small set of components) at a time.

When the ODS contains much data and when the ODS is the focal point of operational processing, it is natural to assume that many analysts and clerks will want to access the ODS. But if enough people wish to access the ODS, if the expected response time is very quick, and if the ODS is actually having update occur against it, in short order the ODS will become a performance bottleneck as illustrated in Figure 2.19. In this scenario, the older application environment will appear to be much more desirable, whatever its shortcomings.

CHANGING TECHNOLOGIES

In addition to performance becoming a concern when the system of record is moved to the ODS, another factor is the change in the underlying technologies. Figure 2.20 demonstrates those changes.

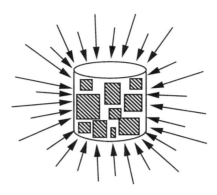

Figure 2.19.   An ODS bottleneck created by too much legacy system data.

When the ODS is in an informational mode and changes are first made to the system of record external to the ODS, the technology for the ODS can be very simple. For all practical purposes, the technology is primarily load and access. But when the system of record—even a small part of it—is shifted to the ODS, the underlying technology changes dramatically. Now it must support a very large and complex infrastructure, even if only a small part of the data in the ODS is the system of record.

If for no other reason than the impact on the underlying technology, very careful consideration must be given to the movement of the system of record into the ODS.

PROCESS ORIENTATION

Perhaps the largest difficulty in the movement of the system of record into the ODS is the change in the orientation of the ODS to process control and management. Figure 2.21 illustrates the difference between having the system of record in the ODS and not having it there.

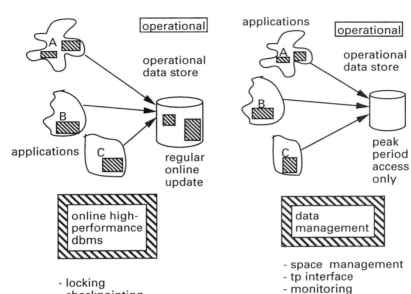

- locking
- checkpointing
- backup
- recovery
- units of work
- backout
- log tapes
- sync points
- commits
- deadlock
- prioritization
- buffer pool management
- block size control
- free space
- free blocks
- overflow detection
- hashing collisions
- online monitors
- scheduling
- prefix resolution
- reorganization

- space management
- tp interface
- monitoring
- loading

Figure 2.20.   The impact of the update feature on ODS—technological considerations.

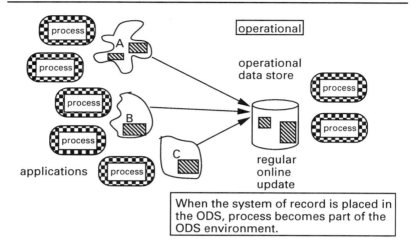

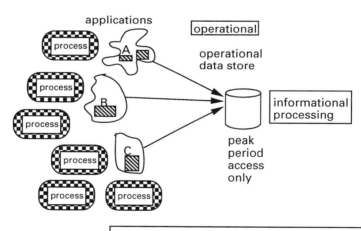

Figure 2.21. The impact of freeing the ODS from the system of record.

As long as the ODS is not part of the system of record, it fulfills a role of informational processing. The ODS serves to integrate and unify data, but essential, interrelated processes exist in the older applications. However, once the system of record becomes embedded in the ODS, there emerges the need to have processing intimately wrapped into the ODS.

This seemingly subtle, insignificant shift in the location of process has complex and far-reaching consequences. For one thing, the whole demeanor of processing changes as soon as the shift is made. The process in the older application environment has (not surprisingly!) an application flavor. But the processes that occur in the ODS have a distinctly corporate flavor. The conflict comes where part of the process in the older applications overlaps with the newly constructed process in the ODS. This problem with a change in the demeanor of processing is very difficult to resolve and is indeed one of the major difficulties in the implementation of reengineering.

METADATA IN THE ODS

Metadata in the data warehouse environment has proven to be a critical component. When the DSS analyst is charged with a task, the first place the DSS analyst turns is the metadata, because this allows the DSS analyst to be proactive in the pursuit of information.

Metadata is likewise invaluable to the user of the ODS. Figure 2.22 shows metadata in the ODS. Metadata allows the clerk or the analyst using the ODS to determine the most likely place to look for information in the ODS. Metadata in the ODS identifies:

- what is in the ODS,
- what the system of record is,

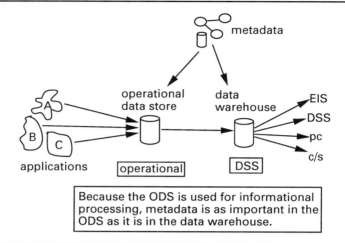

Because the ODS is used for informational
processing, metadata is as important in the
ODS as it is in the data warehouse.

Figure 2.22.   The importance of metadata in the ODS.

- what transformations are made to the data as it passes into the ODS, and
- how ODS data relates to other ODS data.

BUILDING THE ODS

The ODS is best built a small step at a time, in an iterative fashion. The ODS should not be built in massive, large components. There is every likelihood that there will be changes in the ODS—the structure of data, its source, the transformations that are made, and so on—once the ODS is constructed. Therefore, it is a risky strategy to build the ODS in large steps.

Figure 2.23 shows the recommended pattern of building the ODS. We see that on day 1 there is some small amount of data populated into the ODS. More data is populated on day 2. As time progresses, the data in the ODS becomes more and more voluminous and more and more robust.

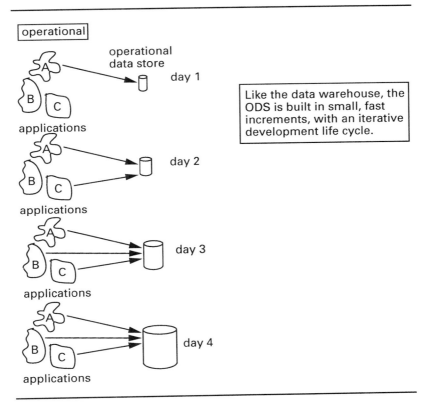

Figure 2.23. Example of building the ODS.

The ODS is built in terms of integrated subject areas. The subject areas come from the corporate data model. The major entities identified in the data model form the foundation for the subject areas in the ODS. Some of the typical major subject areas are customer, activity, supplier, and vendor.

ODS AND EIS

The ODS forms a foundation for operational information processing. There is a difference between the informational processing in the ODS and the informational processing found in the data warehouse. The informational processing found in the ODS is for the clerical community making detailed, up-to-the-second decisions. There is a secondary audience for informational processing in the ODS and that is the manager who is making corporatewide, up-to-the-second decisions, such as in purchasing, reordering, restocking, and product manufacturing.

The type of informational decision being made out of the data warehouse is quite different. The data warehouse is used for long-term, analytical processing. The data warehouse serves primarily the management community looking at the larger perspective.

Nowhere does the difference between the information-processing capabilities of the ODS and of the data warehouse

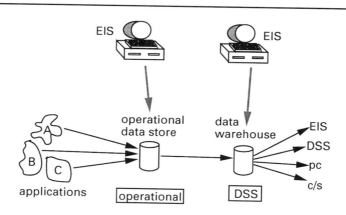

EIS has applicability to both the ODS and the data warehouse. But the use of EIS is quite different in each environment.

Figure 2.24. EIS in the ODS and the data warehouse.

show up more clearly than in the use of EIS. Figure 2.24 shows that EIS can be used for both. When EIS is used in the ODS, EIS is aimed at managers who have to make up-to-the-second decisions. When EIS is used in the data warehouse, the analysis created out of the EIS is used to make long-term, directional decisions.

ODS AND PARALLEL PROCESSING

One form of arrangement of computer processing is called *parallel processing*. Parallel processing allows the workload of a computer to be divided over multiple processors. By dividing the workload, multiple processors can be brought to bear on a single problem.

The parallel approach is especially applicable to the ODS environment because when data is needed it is needed quickly, and the parallel approach allows it to be accessed quickly; and because the quick summary of data can be accommodated easily by a parallel arrangement. Figure 2.25 shows that the parallel arrangement of data fits very nicely with the needs of ODS processing.

HOW CURRENT IS CURRENT?

One of the characteristics of the ODS is that it contains data that is current and near current. *Current* data is obvious: It is data that is accurate as of the moment of access. But what kind of time lag can we tolerate and still allow data to be called *near current*? Figure 2.26 illustrates the dilemma.

The amount of data that is considered to be near current is a function of many things:

- how much data is being considered (the more data there is, the shorter the time span);

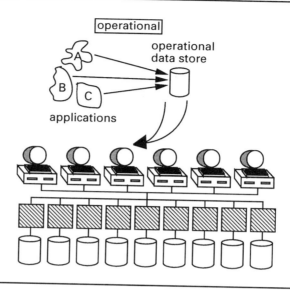

Figure 2.25.   The fit between the ODS and parallel technology.

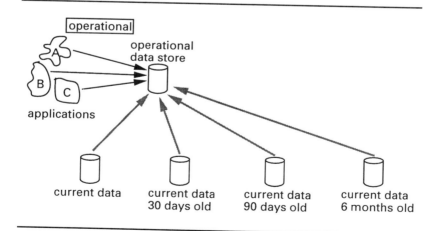

Figure 2.26.   Current and near-current data for the ODS.

- the usage of the near-current data (some businesses have a need for old data, other businesses have very little need for old data);
- the past history of the organization;
- the technology the ODS is positioned on;
- the expected response time of the user (the faster the response time, the shorter the time span);
- the amount of detail being kept, and so forth.

What is near current to one organization is old history to another organization.

PROCESSING WINDOWS

One of the common ways that the ODS is managed is through the creation and management of different processing windows. Figure 2.27 shows that throughout the day there are very different types of processing that are run in the ODS. At odd hours the ODS has massive bulk, sequential load processing executed against it. During the prime hours of the day, the ODS is available for information analytical processing. The "clearing of the decks" (i.e., the removal of nightly batch sequential processing from the windows of analysis during the day) is an essential part of the operation of the ODS environment.

MONITORING THE ODS

An important ongoing activity of the ODS is the ongoing monitoring of the usage of the data found in the ODS. The more usage data receives, the more important it is. Conversely, the less usage data receives, the less important the data is. In fact, if ODS data starts to be used very infrequently, it can actually be removed from the ODS environment. Figure 2.28 shows the results of the ongoing monitoring of ODS data.

There is one exception to this rule, and that is the case

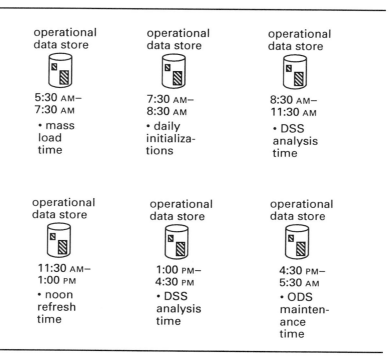

Figure 2.27. Sectioning the day for loading and using the ODS.

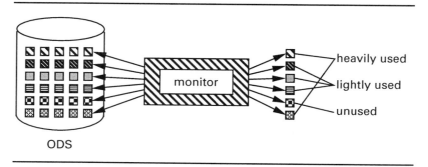

Figure 2.28. Monitoring the ODS for utilization.

where ODS data is infrequently used, but where, once used, the data is extremely important. Occasionally, some data has importance well beyond its actual usage. To keep infrequently used data in the ODS is a business decision, not a technological or design consideration.

Usually the monitoring of the usage of ODS data is done on a table by table basis. Given the monitors of database management decisions, it is very difficult to achieve a breakdown of usage lower than the table level.

DATA RELATIONSHIPS IN THE ODS

One of the most important aspects of any database environment is that of data relationships. Data relationships are those that allow one table to be related to another table, or one unit of data in a table to be related to another unit of data in another table. Data relationships are as important in the ODS as they are anywhere else.

However, the implementation of data relationships in the ODS takes on a very different flavor than in the classical operational environment. As long as the ODS does not take on any aspect of the system of record, data relationships are implemented in the form of an artifact. Once the ODS starts to contain all or part of the system of record, then the ODS must implement a data relationship in the classical form of referential integrity.

(For an in-depth discussion of data relationships and artifacts in an informational environment, please refer to the Prism Solutions Tech Topic on data relationships in the data warehouse environment.)

WHY THE ODS IS IMPORTANT

The ODS is an important architectural entity unto itself. It has its own place and its own constituency. The ODS in many ways looks like and feels like a data warehouse. In some ways, the ODS can be considered to be an offshoot or hybrid version of the data warehouse. But mixing the data warehouse and the ODS—in usage, in design, in concept—can be a very dangerous mistake. The effective DSS analyst *must* be clear as to what environment is under consideration.

SUMMARY

This chapter has explored the ODS in depth. The ODS is part of a larger architecture, with certain similarities to and differences from the data warehouse. The ODS may or may not contain part of the system of record. When the ODS starts to contain some or all of the system of record, there are many design and technological implications. When the ODS does not contain the system of record, it is used strictly for informational processing.

The ODS contains nearly all detail data. The summary data contained in the ODS is accurate only as of the moment of access. The ODS has a peculiar affinity for parallel processing.

3

The Data Warehouse and the ODS

Each of the architectural constructs—the data warehouse and the ODS—has its own characteristics and peculiarities. Together they form the basic features of an architecture designed to meet the informational needs of the corporation.

Effective informational processing and the use of the information architecture starts with an understanding of the components of the architecture. Trying to do processing that is inappropriate to one or the other level of processing within the architecture precludes success.

There is an architecture for informational processing that features the data warehouse and another architecture that features both the data warehouse and the ODS. Figure 3.1 illustrates these two variations of the informational architecture.

Both architectures are valid—neither invalidates the place and purpose of the other. Some types of systems will fit one architecture and other types of systems will fit the other architecture.

In general, where there is no need for operational inte-

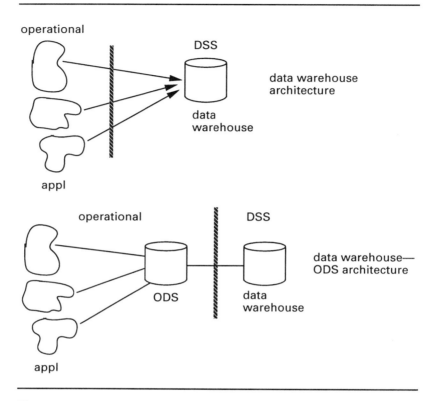

Figure 3.1.   Two valid architecture.

gration, the data warehouse–based architecture is optimal. And in circumstances where there is a need for operational integration in the face of older, unintegrated legacy systems, the data warehouse/ODS architecture is optimal.

  An example of an environment where there is no need for operational integration is the case where different systems manage the worldwide financial concerns for a multinational corporation. Figure 3.2 illustrates such a case, where there are basic systems that are used for the financial management of the corporations concerns in Europe, America, and the Far East. These disparate operational applications and systems

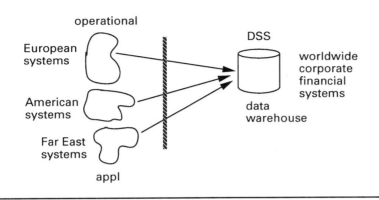

Figure 3.2.   An example where integration may not happen.

probably have very little in common in the way of hardware, software, or applications. Each of the geographical units manages its business as if it was autonomous. On an up-to-the-second basis there is no need to have a corporate financial picture. Under these conditions there is no need for an ODS.

But consider the environment found in Figure 3.3, which shows that there are base legacy applications for a financial institute for loans processing, savings processing, and trust

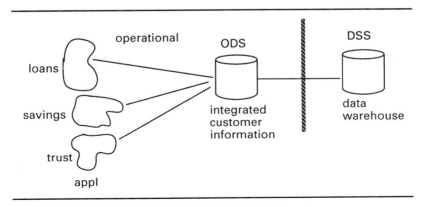

Figure 3.3.   Where an ODS makes sense.

processing. These applications have been written separately and have little or no integration among them. However, there is a business need to understand who a customer is and there is a need to have the customer's information be accurate up to the second. In order to achieve integration across the older legacy systems, data is integrated from the different applications into an ODS. At the ODS, the various aspects of the customer begin to merge and a unified customer perspective is created from the data gleaned from the various legacy applications. Operational, application data is fed into the ODS as soon as possible. The ODS forms a basis for making up-to-the-second customer decisions in an integrated manner. In this case, having only a data warehouse would not suffice to serve the needs of the corporation.

Note that building and maintaining an ODS does nothing to negate the need for a data warehouse. After the very current ODS data ages, it is passed to the data warehouse. Once in the data warehouse, the integrated data forms a basis for managerial decisions and managerial treatment of an account or a customer.

When there is no ODS, the interface to the operational, legacy world is a rather complex, multifaceted one. But when the data warehouse is fed from an ODS, the interface is usually straightforward.

In many ways, the ODS and the data warehouse are similar. In fact, the temptation is to try to merge them together. But, as we have seen, for a variety of reasons it makes no sense to merge the ODS and the data warehouse into a single structure. Figure 3.4 shows this error in design.

DYNAMICS OF UPDATE

Both the data warehouse and the ODS are fed by the system of record. In the case where the architecture contains only the data warehouse, the legacy applications feed the data warehouse. In the architecture where there is both the ODS

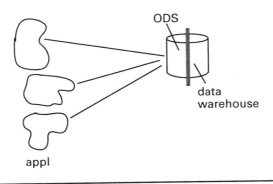

Figure 3.4.   A combination that does not make sense.

and the data warehouse, the system of record for the ODS is the legacy applications and the system of record for the data warehouse is the ODS (in almost every case).

From the standpoint of the speed with which data flows out of the system of record, there is a very different notion of the flow of data into the ODS and the data warehouse from the system of record. Figure 3.5 depicts the difference in the rate of flow of data into the two environments.

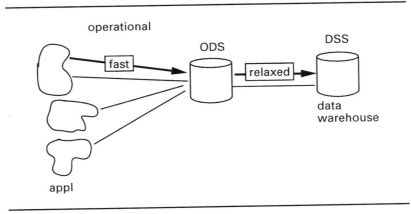

Figure 3.5.   The differences in rate of refreshment.

Data flows into the ODS in a very timely fashion. Data flows into the data warehouse in a very relaxed fashion. Typically, the amount of time that passes from the moment a change is made to the operational legacy environment until the change is reflected in the ODS is a matter of minutes or even hours. Anywhere from ten minutes to four hours is normal.

When data passes into the ODS very quickly, the trapping of the change in the operational legacy systems environment must be done at the application level. When there is a time lag of a few hours or more, the trapping of the change can occur either at the application level or at the log tape or journal level.

When data is passed to the data warehouse, the time lag is often 24 hours or longer. There is a marked difference between the need for currency of data between the ODS and the data warehouse.

The difference in the currency of data between the two environments shows up in many ways. The technology required to manage a very short time lag is much more expensive and complex than the technology required to manage a relaxed time lag. The usage of the data is likewise very different. If there is a need for very current data, the need must be met in the ODS. If, on the other hand, there is no need for very current data, then the need can be met in the data warehouse.

The differing needs for the currency of data play a role in many design aspects of the ODS and the data warehouse.

SUMMARY DATA

One of the more important differences between the two environments is in how summarization is handled. In the ODS, summarization is done on an as-needed basis and is accurate only as of the moment the summary is created. In addition, it is very difficult to recreate (or even audit) summary data created from the ODS. For these reasons, summary data is not stored for any great amount of time in the ODS.

The data warehouse, on the other hand, is full of summary data. The data warehouse contains both summary and detailed data. The data warehouse summary data can be audited and recreated easily. Of course, new summarizations may be created in the data warehouse. Upon creation, they may be discarded or may be stored for future use. The summary that occurs in the data warehouse is primarily for the management of the company.

Figure 3.6 illustrates the difference between the summaries occurring in the two environments.

Summary at the ODS level is done dynamically. A program is put into execution to calculate the number of trades that have been made for a broker as of 1:35 P.M. The pro-

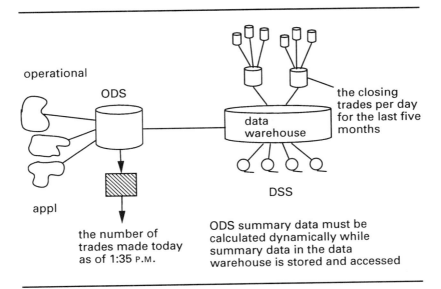

Figure 3.6.   Dynamic summary versus stored summary.

gram accesses the appropriate data in the ODS and does the required calculation. After the calculation is used, it is discarded.

On the other hand, summary information in the data warehouse is regularly calculated and stored as a part of the data warehouse. When someone desires to access the data warehouse summary data it is a simple matter to retrieve the summary data. The data warehouse summary data reflects data calculated over time and forms a foundation for long-term visions of management. Trend analysis is done based on the long time spans of data housed in the data warehouse.

DIFFERENT USER COMMUNITIES

The several components of the architecture have different user communities, each which has a unique perspective of how the data is to be used. Figure 3.7 shows the different user communities that are found at the various levels of the architecture.

At the operational application level are found the most clerical of the users. The clerical users desire to answer very detailed and immediate questions. The focus of the clerical community is the day-to-day activities of the running of the corporation. In many cases, the clerical community operates from a basis of unintegrated application systems. For the purposes of serving the immediate needs of the organization, having an unintegrated foundation of application data may suffice. Very short-term decisions with a narrow perspective are being made based on the data found at this level of the architecture.

At the ODS level is found a community of users that are concerned with the immediate operations of the enterprise, but are operating at a higher level than the clerical application–based users. The ODS user needs an integrated, corpo-

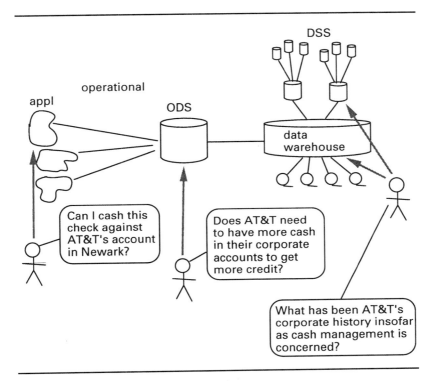

Figure 3.7.   Decision-making needs.

rate perspective, and the ODS provides this foundation. The data found in the ODS is truly integrated. The ODS data may not be quite as current as the application data, but the data is nevertheless fresh. The ODS data serves as a basis for understanding operational activities at a corporate level. Short-term, corporatewide decisions are being made from data found at this level of the architecture.

The users of the data warehouse are the long-term decision makers of the corporation. Looking for patterns of data across many activities, or looking for trends across long periods of time is the objective of the community of users served by the data warehouse. The data in the data warehouse must be integrated and must be historical to support the needs of this analytical, management-focused user. Long-term decisions affecting the directions of the business are made from the data warehouse.

METADATA IN THE ARCHITECTURE

An important feature of the informational architecture is that of metadata. In its simplest form, metadata is merely data about data. But in the larger architecture, metadata takes on a much more important and complex role than is suggested by this simple definition. In a sense, it is metadata that is the glue that binds the architecture together.

Figure 3.8 shows the role of metadata in the context of the larger informational architecture. Here, there are four major types of metadata in the information architecture. There is metadata for the legacy application environment, there is metadata for the ODS environment, there is metadata for the data warehouse, and there is metadata for

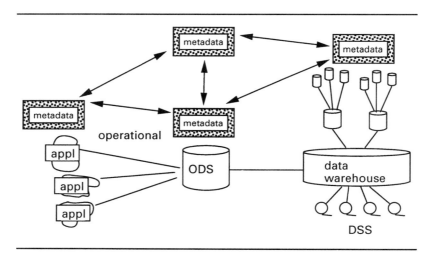

Figure 3.8.   Example of different levels of metadata.

the entire architecture. The metadata serves different communities with different agendas at each level.

The metadata for the architecture is spread over different parts of the architecture and takes on a form peculiar to the architecture. In addition, there is the free flow of metadata from one part of the architecture to another part.

Operational legacy systems metadata is shown in Figure 3.9. Operational legacy systems metadata is typically found in a data dictionary or copy directory. Operational legacy systems metadata includes physical descriptions of files (i.e., data layouts), common code, definition of relationships between tables, control block definition, indexing information, and so forth. The metadata found at the operational legacy level is oriented toward physical design. In many cases, the metadata is scattered over a variety of directories, libraries, and dictionaries, and is entered into the dictionary at the inception of a project and never updated thereafter, thus circumventing its usefulness.

As a rule, operational legacy metadata is used in a reactive fashion, as a byproduct of the building of an application. The consistency, currency, and breadth of operational legacy systems data prevents it from being used in a proactive fashion.

The ODS metadata often resides on a dictionary. Figure 3.10 shows ODS metadata. As a rule, the ODS metadata

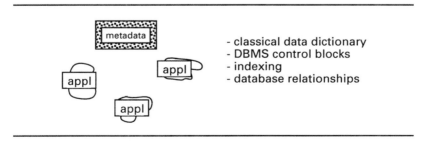

Figure 3.9.   The classical data dictionary.

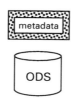

- warehouse management
- database structure
- system-of-record definition

Figure 3.10.   The ODS data dictionary.

tends to be much more up to date and platformed on a new repository technology (because the ODS is a relatively new architectural construct). ODS metadata consists of descriptive information. In addition, the ODS metadata contains the definition of the system of record, the logic used in the transformation of the system of record into the ODS, metrics relevant to the ODS, and so forth. The ODS data is used in a proactive fashion by the DSS analyst in the search and interpretation of the contents of the ODS. In addition, the ODS metadata is used in a passive fashion by the developer and database administrator.

Data warehouse metadata, shown in Figure 3.11, serves both the data architecture community and the DSS analysis community.

The data warehouse metadata contains descriptive information, system-of-record (source systems) information, transformation information, and other types of metadata. All data warehouse data must be "versioned." The versioning of data warehouse metadata simply means that the metadata be kept over time. In other words, as a change is made to the data warehouse, the change should be recorded along with previous changes, not replacing them. It is not enough to store only current metadata in the data warehouse; the history of metadata must be stored. This is because data is stored for a long time in the data warehouse and the metadata that ac-

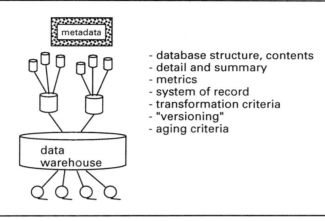

- database structure, contents
- detail and summary
- metrics
- system of record
- transformation criteria
- "versioning"
- aging criteria

Figure 3.11. The data warehouse metadata.

companies the raw data in many ways is as important as the actual data warehouse data itself.

There are other types of metadata that make sense in the data warehouse, such as metrics information, profile information, purge criteria description, monitoring information, and scheduling information.

The corporate metadata sits above the other types of metadata. The corporate metadata shows how the different levels of data relate, and contains such things as modeling information, key structure information, and definitions of data. Figure 3.12 illustrates corporate metadata, for enterprisewide planning and design.

Figure 3.13 shows that there are different communities using metadata throughout the architecture. The flow of data should be unrestricted from one level to another.

THE PLATFORMS

The informational architecture is supported by a wide variety of platforms. It is very unusual to have only one type of

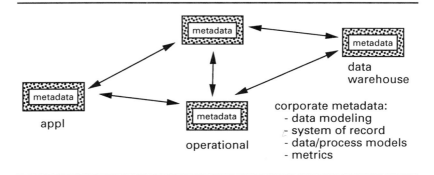

Figure 3.12. Corporate metadata.

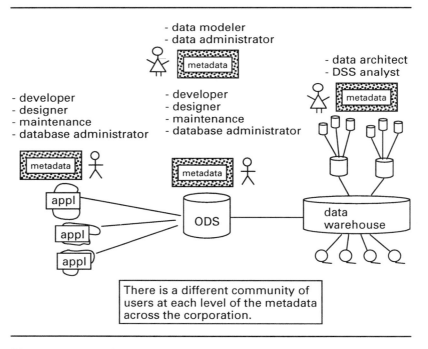

Figure 3.13. Community of users and levels of metadata.

platform to support a given level of the architecture. The types of platforms that are commonly found are:

- the parallel platform,
- the mainframe platform,
- the client/server platform, and
- the PC or workstation platform.

Figure 3.14 illustrates how the platforms of technology typically support the different levels of the informational architecture. At the operational, legacy systems application level are found the mainframe and the client/server environment. The ODS level is typically supported by the parallel, mainframe or client/server environment. The data warehouse employs a wide diversity of platforms, depending on the level of data within the data warehouse. Highly summarized data warehouse data is found on PC, workstation, and EIS platforms. Lightly summarized data warehouse data is

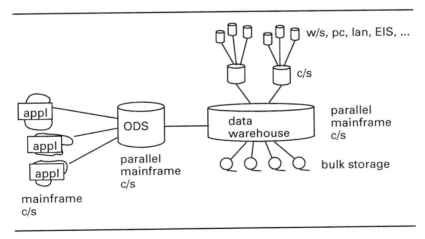

Figure 3.14.   Platforms at different levels.

housed on the client/server environment. The current detail level of data of the data warehouse is platformed on a parallel platform, a mainframe platform, or a client/server platform. The older detail of the data warehouse is housed on a bulk storage platform.

Two components of the architecture—the ODS and the current detail portion of the data warehouse—are particularly sensitive to the platforms on which they are placed because of several factors:

- the volume of data that is found on them, and
- the cost of storage and manipulation of data.

Given the volume of data that is found in the ODS and the current level of detail of the data warehouse, very careful consideration must be made as to the platform. In particular, these two architectural constructs often require quick, direct access of small units of data. When there is a need for the management of very large amounts of data in a direct fashion, the parallel approach to the management of data is optimal (indeed, in some cases the parallel approach may be the only technologically viable option). Unfortunately, the cost of the parallel approach is also the most expensive. So the volume of data that will be managed in a parallel fashion must be carefully gauged. It is a mistake to carelessly load huge amounts of data onto a parallel platform for either the ODS or the current level of detail for the data warehouse. On the other hand, if there is a need to manage large amounts of data directly, then a parallel approach may be the only alternative.

However, when there is not much need for direct access of data in the ODS and/or the current level of detail of the data warehouse, or where the volume of data is not overwhelming, then the mainframe or the distributed client/server approach may be a good solution in terms of platforms. As a rule, it costs less to manage modest amounts of data on a mainframe or a client/server than it does on a parallel platform. In the same vein, it costs less to manage small amounts of data on the client/server environment than it does for the mainframe environment.

The optimal platform for any given company for any given component of the informational architecture is determined by many factors, such as the size of the company, the nature of the business of the company, the past technological history of the company, the budget, and the amount of data to be managed.

SUMMARY

The effective use of the informational architecture begins with an in-depth understanding of the architectures into which the data warehouse and the ODS fit. The data warehouse architecture does not negate the validity of the data warehouse/ODS architecture, nor vice versa. Each architecture has its appropriate place.

The components of the architecture are held together by metadata. Different metadata applies to each level of the architecture. In addition, there is a free flow of metadata from one part of the informational architecture to another. Different platforms house the different levels of the architecture.

4

Using the Data Warehouse: The Manager's Perspective

The data warehouse and the architectures associated with it provide a target for coming to grips with the many variables and challenges confronting information systems management today. In a word, the data warehouse allows management to consider issues in context. Without the framework of the data warehouse and the associated architectures, trying to make sense of the diverse issues becomes an almost impossible task.

Figure 4.1 illustrates the different data warehouse architectures and the role they play in shaping management's decisions. It is said that any current and any wind is satisfactory for a boat without a rudder and without a destination. The IS manager without an understanding of architecture is like the drifting aimless boat. This chapter will address how the data warehouse and architecture provide context in which to do effective information processing to the manager of information systems.

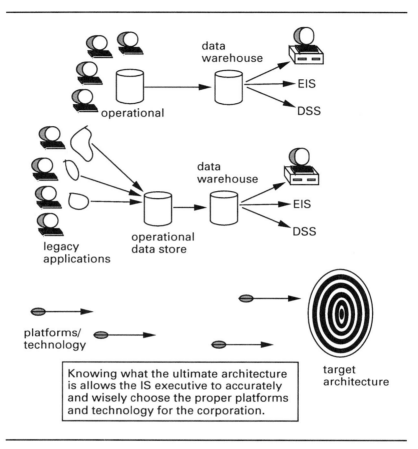

Figure 4.1. Platforms on technology fit architecture.

MANAGING STORAGE

The management of the growth of the demand for storage at first glance appears to be an almost trivial subject. It is not. The simplest aspect of managing the growth of storage management is that of managing costs and selecting storage. Once the basic storage technology has been selected and installed, the issues of orderly growth and the introduction of different storage technologies at the appropriate time become germane to the organization. It is a temptation for a manager to buy the most expensive and fastest storage because fast and expensive storage has the capability of serving many needs very efficiently. Unfortunately, the organization's demand for high-performance storage outstrips the supply of the storage, whatever the plans of the organization. At some point, the myth that "storage is getting cheaper and more plentiful all the time" becomes unmasked. However plentiful storage is, the demand exceeds the budget allocated for the supply.

The issue of when to bring in newer storage technologies plays an important role in the type of systems that can be built. A manager can constrain systems development simply by controlling the storage in the shop.

When management reaches the point of maturity and realizes that judicious acquisition of storage and selective deployment of different types of storage technologies are an important part of the larger picture of information systems, the importance of the notion of architecture becomes apparent.

Figure 4.2 illustrates how storage needs and the growth of storage needs differ across the architected environment. The operational environment has a need for fairly large amounts of expensive high-performance storage. The growth of the need for operational storage is steady. Once the operational environment is clearly separated from the DSS environment, as shown in the figure, the need for high-performance storage grows in a stable and controlled manner.

But in the case where operational processing is indiscriminately mixed in with DSS processing, it is hard to ferret out the difference between operational growth and DSS growth.

Once the two environments are separated in accordance with the architecture, there is a corresponding growth in the

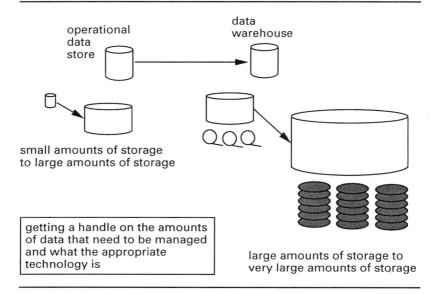

operational data store

data warehouse

small amounts of storage to large amounts of storage

getting a handle on the amounts of data that need to be managed and what the appropriate technology is

large amounts of storage to very large amounts of storage

Figure 4.2.   Quality of data impacts technology.

need for storage in the data warehouse. The storage technology found in the data warehouse is for slower, less expensive storage than that found in the operational environment. In addition, for the more detailed, older regions of the data warehouse, slow, bulk storage technology is optimal. Without the notion of architecture, the needs for different storage technologies and the differences in the growth rates are not so cleanly categorized. Architecture allows the manager to separate the types of data and processing and to map the data and processing to appropriate storage technology.

One of the reasons why different storage technologies are appropriate to different parts of the architecture is because of the difference between and the need for fast direct access and the need for moderately fast direct access coupled with the need for efficient sequential access. Figure 4.3 shows that

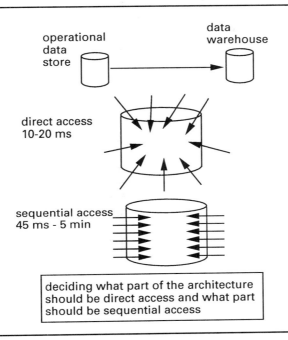

operational
data
store

data
warehouse

direct access
10-20 ms

sequential access
45 ms - 5 min

deciding what part of the architecture
should be direct access and what part
should be sequential access

Figure 4.3.   Direct access versus sequential.

some storage technology is organized for very quick direct access of a single unit of data. Usually, this technology is expensive and does not handle massive sequential access efficiently. The needs of the operational, transaction environment and the ODS fit very well with this type of storage technology.

A second type of storage technology is technology that allows data to be accessed directly but also allows data to be sequentially accessed. This technology—a *mixed* direct access/sequential access technology—is less expensive than very-high-performance technology (although it is still not cheap). Mixed sequential/direct access technology is best suited for the current detailed component of the data warehouse (although it is quite versatile and can be used elsewhere). In some environments the mixed storage technology is also used for the operational environment.

Other types of storage technology include bulk storage of data, which is the least inexpensive and allows massive amounts of data to be stored. But it is relatively slow in its access. Bulk storage of data is good for old detail data in the data warehouse and other archiving needs, such as auditing.

Without the concept of architecture, the IS manager has a difficult time making sense of the different needs of the organization when it comes to managing storage. Architecture provides a context—a *Framework*—for the management of the storage needs of the organization.

DETAILED DATA/SUMMARY DATA

A basic problem facing every IS manager is that of storing summary data. Whether or not to store summary data has been debated for as long as there have been information systems. The advocates of structured programming—the original proponents of discipline in the development process—have long maintained that no summary data need be stored. The theory was that summary data should be calculated each time it is needed, because the summary data would always be accurate as of the moment of calculation. But the end-user organization—in their spreadsheets and their EIS—have stored summary data for many years now. End users have recognized that recalculating summary data every time it is needed is not feasible. Architecture allows the IS manager to understand the issues and resolve the conflict between the two schools of thought. Figure 4.4 shows that there is a well-defined place for different kinds of summary data in the data warehouse.

The detail data in the data warehouse provides the basis

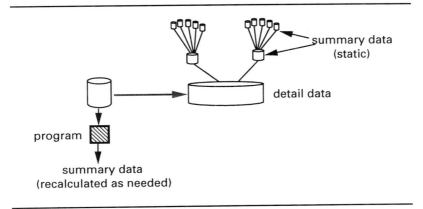

Figure 4.4.   Planning for summary data and detailed data.

for calculation of static summary data. The static summary data in the data warehouse is available for regular access and analysis by the DSS analyst. Furthermore, the static summary data in the data warehouse can be recalculated if need be.

But there is another type of summary data in the IS environment—dynamic data that is calculated on a moment's notice. Dynamic summary data is calculated from detail data found in the ODS or in the operational legacy applications. The dynamic summary data that is created on the fly has only a limited lifespan of usefulness and is not stored for any great length of time. The structured advocates of yesteryear referred to dynamic summary data when they stated that summary data should not be stored. Static data warehouse summary data certainly should be stored as a regular part of the environment.

The context of architecture gives the IS manager the framework needed to make sense of the basic conflict in philosophies that regularly arises in the IS environment over summary data.

MANAGING THE BUDGETARY PROCESS

Another very important aspect of the IS function is that of managing the budget. It is through the budgetary process that the political lines of the corporation are drawn. Through the budgetary lines the information processing organization prospers or shrinks.

In the early years of building the IS organization the budget for technology was so small that a fair amount of money was available for R&D. There was little need for tight budgetary control in the formative years. But the IS/technology budget has grown so large that today the expenditures on IS are watched closely from the highest levels of the corporation. No longer does IS spending represent a small fraction of corporate revenue.

As long as there is no notion of architecture, managing the IS budget is a daunting task. But the formalization and acceptance of architecture arms the IS executive with the framework needed to effectively manage the budget. Figure 4.5 shows the simplifying effect of architecture on the budget. The budgetary process can be broken into finite and

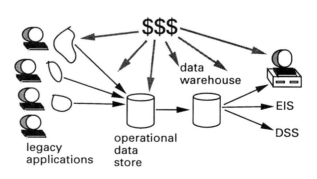

Figure 4.5. Managing the budget.

well-defined components in the face of the natural divisions that occur as a result of architecture. Certain parts of the budgetary process naturally fall outside the domain of the IS organization. Other parts of the budgetary process fall directly into the hands of the IS organization. The dividing line between what parts of the budget should and should not be IS controlled becomes clear in the face of architecture.

IS usually has little or no influence on the budget on the right-hand side of the architecture. The end user manages the budget and the world of informational processing outside of the data warehouse.

There is a central IS organization that manages the data warehouse and the ODS. This centralized IS function has its own separate budget. And for the remainder of IS, the different application groups manage the development and maintenance budget required for the building of legacy applications and the maintenance of those applications.

By breaking the world of information processing into its component parts, the budgetary process is broken into finite components as well, and as a result becomes manageable.

MANAGING GROWTH

In the same vein as the management of the budget comes the prediction and management of growth of technology. Different parts of the IS environment grow at different rates and with a different level of criticality. The notion of architecture breaks the complex IS environment up into different components. Once the components are divided, they can be analyzed in isolation from each other. Figure 4.6 shows the growth that occurs in the different parts of the IS environment.

Growth in the legacy systems environment occurs because of a change in business circumstances, and to a lesser extent because of the complexity of maintaining old systems. On occasion, as a new legacy system is added, growth occurs

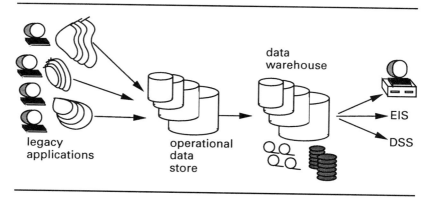

data
warehouse

EIS

DSS

legacy
applications

operational
data
store

Figure 4.6. Predicting and managing growth.

simply because of the complexity of adding a new component
to an environment that is ill-prepared to accept it. For the
most part, legacy systems growth is predictable.

Growth occurs in the ODS environment because of the
new opportunities that are afforded by doing online corporate
integrated processing. The growth in the ODS environment
occurs spontaneously, and as a result is quite unpredictable.
Given that the ODS does not contain data with a lengthy time
horizon and that the ODS does not permanently store summary data, the growth of storage is usually small and unpredictable. However, because of the dynamic needs for processor
power, the growth of CPU resources is variable and quite
unpredictable.

Growth in the data warehouse is explosive. Driving the
growth in the data warehouse is the corporate ability to effectively and efficiently do informational processing. Most
organizations have never been able to do effective and efficient informational processing, so the motivation for growth
in the data warehouse is very strong.

Since the data warehouse contains both summary data
and a long time horizon of data (i.e., five to ten years of data),

the growth of storage is dramatic and never-ending in the data warehouse. In the early days of the data warehouse the demand for processing power grows along with the growth of storage. Interestingly, the growth of processing power for the data warehouse environment remains constant after the data warehouse reaches a state of early maturity. Once the end user starts to take data warehouse data off to other processors, the demand for more processing power abates.

Most organizations discover the advantages of informational processing very late in the day, so that there is a latent demand that is quite large and unpredictable.

The growth in the end user/informational sector (i.e., the EIS, DSS, reporting sector) is likewise unpredictable. This growth occurs on a user-by-user basis: for a while, one user grows rapidly, then stops. Then for a while no users experience growth. Then two users experience growth simultaneously, and so forth. There is no regular or observable pattern to the growth that occurs in this sector. The motivation for growth in the end-user sector is driven on an end-user-at-a-time basis.

Without the context of architecture, the IS manager has a difficult time coming to grips with the different rates of growth and the causes of growth, and in discerning an orderly pattern of progression for the organization.

CHANGING PLATFORMS/CHANGING TECHNOLOGIES

One of the gripping decisions facing every IS manager is that of changing platforms or technologies. There are a variety of reasons why occasionally a change in platforms and/or technology needs to be considered:

- Current vendors of technology no longer supply what is needed.

- Older technology cannot be extended any more.
- New opportunities arise with newer technology.
- Organizations are being merged.
- The growth rate has exceeded any previous expectation.
- Older technologies were never designed to meet today's needs.

Every IS organization eventually faces the day when decisions need to be made regarding the replacement or the extension of an existing technology.

The replacement of platforms and/or technology is fraught with difficulties. The cost of replacement is not trivial, the cost of placing the new technology in the organization can be frightening, the disruption to the organization in the uprooting of older technology (whatever its shortcomings!) is not something that is ever taken lightly, and so forth. Simply stated, the introduction of a new platform and/or a new technology along with the dissolution of older platforms and/or technologies is never a pleasant prospect.

The context of architecture allows the IS manager to understand where the disruptions will be and how best to replace the older technology. Figure 4.7 shows a simple consideration of the replacement of mainframe technology with parallel technology in the face of the architected environment.

The notion of architecture allows the IS manager to consider the different parts of the organization's technology in isolation from each other. In doing so, the decision for technology can be narrowed down to a finite set of considerations. However, when the technological environment is not considered as an architecture, with its cohesive components, then the tight intertwinings of the unarchitected environment make evaluating any new technology very difficult. The different older technologies become so tightly interwoven that they can never be extricated.

The context of architecture allows the IS manager to be

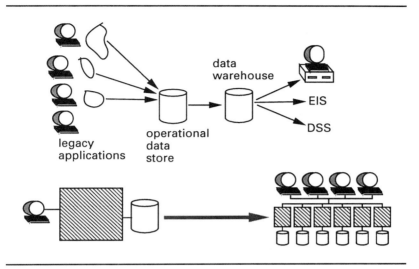

Figure 4.7.   Changing platforms.

able to consider how older platforms and/or technologies can be decoupled with a minimum of disruption.

INFORMATIONAL PROCESSING

Perhaps the most elusive and at the same time most potentially rewarding aspect of architecture is the enablement of the organization to do informational processing. The stories of other companies doing informational processing and of how informational processing has contributed in a very positive fashion to the bottom line are legion. Yet the success stories always seem to be happening elsewhere.

It is through architecture that the IS manager unlocks the organization's older legacy, production environment to the accomplishment of effective informational processing, as illustrated in Figure 4.8.

Later chapters will explore the many ways that informa-

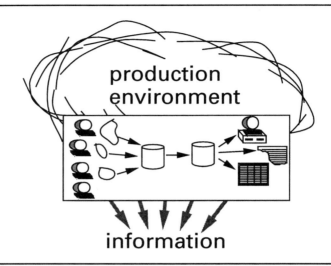

Figure 4.8.   Basic architecture serves planner.

tion is gleaned from the production environment. In general, it suffices to say that doing effective informational processing from the production, legacy systems environment has proven to be a fiction rather than a fact. For the longest time it was held that superficial techniques such as "masking" operational data, or creating artificial "views" of data was what was needed to achieve informational processing from the basis of legacy systems. It is only after companies realize that they have to get down to the bedrock of production and legacy data and make fundamental changes to that data that informational processing starts to be a reality.

CREATING LINES OF AUTHORITY

A constant problem facing the IS manager is how to organize the many organizational functions that are needed to keep the technology infrastructure from collapsing. Unless care is taken, an organizational structure will be created where there are conflicting goals and missions within the same organization. When different parts of the same organization are at odds with each other the result is confusion and deadlock, with little progress.

At the highest levels of responsibility, architecture suggests that there should be three major organizations—the applications development/maintenance function, the data architecture function, and the end-user/informational function. Figure 4.9 illustrates these major subdivisions of responsibility based on the context of architecture.

The applications/development function has responsibility for the older legacy applications and for new applications that are just being built. The data architecture function has responsibility for the building and operation of the ODS and the data warehouse. The end user has responsibility for processing that occurs once the data leaves the data ware-

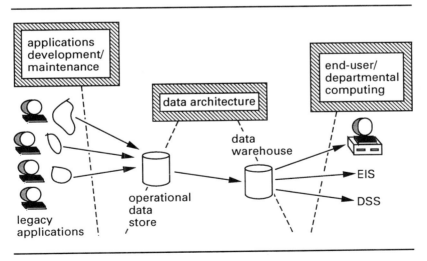

Figure 4.9.   The question of organizational responsibilities.

house. Of course, there will be further divisions of responsibility beneath the functional areas that have been identified. However, delineating the organization along the lines that have been suggested allows the major goals, missions, and expectations of the different organizational divisions to be in alignment. Stated conversely, when there is no definition of responsibility along the lines that have been suggested by architecture, of necessity there will be conflicting goals and objectives within the same organization.

Architecture, then, allows the IS manager to separate the organization into compatible subunits so that responsibility and mission are not confused.

THE REPORTING FUNCTION

If there is no other purpose the notion of architecture serves, architecture very strongly suggests that there should be an organized, methodical way to approach the subject of reporting in the organization. Management can transform the unorganized, catch-as-catch-can approach to reporting typical of the production legacy environment into a well-structured approach toward reporting based on architecture. Figure 4.10 shows how architecture in its larger form is used as a foundation for a reporting architecture. Each of the different parts of the architecture produces its own reports. Detailed, up-to-the-second reports used to satisfy the needs of the clerical community are produced out of the legacy, application environment. Corporatewide, operational reports used for making integrated corporate decisions are produced from the ODS. Both detailed analysis and summary analysis over a long period of time—such as trend analysis—are produced in reports coming out of the data warehouse. And specialized reports peculiar to a particular department are produced out of the end user/departmental portion of the architecture.

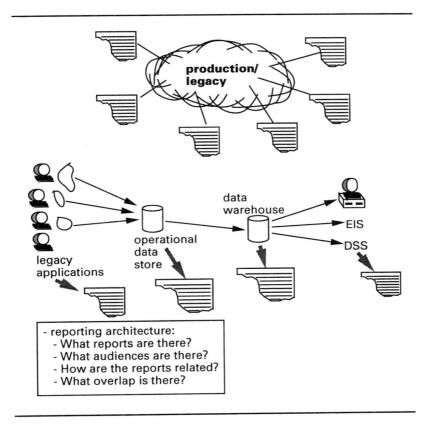

Figure 4.10.   Reporting architecture.

The simple message of the reporting architecture is that there are appropriate places for the achievement of certain types of reporting as well as inappropriate places. When the IS developer tries to build a report inappropriately in the production/legacy environment, there is nothing to signal that an improper design decision has been made. In the production/legacy environment there is no larger design that serves to distinguish one type of reporting from another. But in the architected environment, there is a very clear signal that some types of reports are proper to one function and other types of reports are proper to other functions.

The resulting reporting architecture makes it much simpler for the IS manager to decide the proper place for resources, attention, maintenance, new development, and so on.

ORGANIZATIONAL INTERFACES/STRUCTURES

Just as architecture provides the appropriate context for the organization of different functions, architecture also provides the context for interfaces between the different organizations and functions. Figure 4.11 shows the interface between the different organizational units.

The primary interfaces are between the applications development/maintenance and data architecture functions and between the data architecture and the end-user/departmental functions. The applications/data architecture interface is typified by the data architecture function representing the

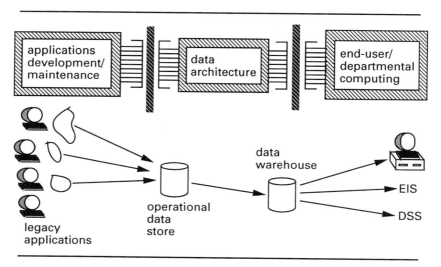

Figure 4.11.   The question of organizational interface.

needs for integration of the organization and the development organization representing the immediate needs for applications development. There is a natural tug of war between these two seemingly conflicting goals. In some cases, there will be an ODS and in other cases there will be no ODS. When there is no ODS, the applications group owns classical requirements-based processing. The only turf given up by the applications group comes in the reporting function when there is a need for integrated reporting across the organization.

The data architecture organization is concerned with the issues of corporate integration. Usually a data model and the definition of the system of record provides the key into the world of applications.

The data architecture/end-user interface is quite different from the applications/data architecture interface. The data architecture/end-user interface is typified by the data architecture organization playing a service role to the end user. The data architecture function in many ways is a "utility" for the needs of the end user. It has the responsibility for teaching the end-user function about the importance of architecture and how to make effective use of it.

In the early days of computation it was thought that only the information professional should be allowed to touch and manipulate technology. But as time has passed and the data architecture organization has matured, there is the notion that the end user should have the right to do whatever processing is appropriate. This change of attitude has had an impact all across the face of the organization. Not least affected has been the organization chart itself.

Consider how the organization chart was arranged in the early days of computing insofar as the roles and responsibilities of computing are concerned. Figure 4.12 shows the classical organization chart. There was one organization—the information systems organization—that was charged with the acquisition and management of technology. Other

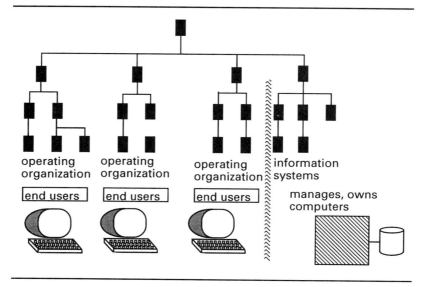

Figure 4.12.   The legacy system organizations structure.

end-user organizations could use technology, but were only allowed to be a passive viewer. No development or other ownership of technology was even considered.

Over time the ownership of computing changed. In fact, the ownership of data, at least in part, passed into the operating organization, out of the hands of the information systems staff. Figure 4.13 shows the progression over time from the perspective of the organization chart.

Soon all the information systems staff owned was a collection of central transaction processing systems. Once the data was processed centrally, the data or derivatives thereof were passed to the operating organization. Once inside the confines of the operating organization, the data formed the foundation of systems private to the operating organization.

From the standpoint of ownership of data, the operating department was content with this arrangement. But at a

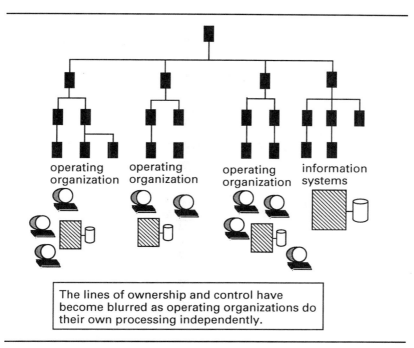

The lines of ownership and control have become blurred as operating organizations do their own processing independently.

Figure 4.13.   The question of ownership and control.

higher corporate level there was great dissatisfaction with this arrangement. The result of spreading data and technology across the organization chart was that each operating function reported its results entirely independently from any other operating function. The corporation had many conflicting analyses (and consequently, many conflicting decisions). The result was a "spider web" of data and information processing. (See the References for a list of books giving a complete description of the growth of the spider web environment.) After a period of time, the ownership of data and technology by the different operating groups became a burden to the corporation.

Once the difficulties of each operating organization own-

ing and managing their own information processing departments began to place a hardship on the corporation, the concept of architecture was used to restore order to information
processing. Figure 4.14 shows how the concept of architecture
is used to straighten out the organizational mess in which

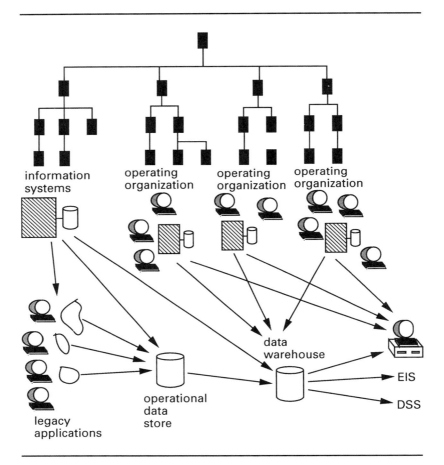

Figure 4.14.   Providing structure to the management of data and
systems across the enterprise.

most corporations find themselves. The old information systems organization becomes the owner of legacy systems, the ODS, and the data warehouse. The operating organizations use data from the data warehouse to run whatever analytical systems they have. The dividing line between what information processing is appropriate and what is inappropriate for an operating organization to manage becomes clear in the face of architecture.

Architecture becomes an essential tool for the IS manager in a corporation struggling with the issues of what is proper and what is improper information processing for the operating organization.

CHANGING THE DEVELOPMENT PROCESS

When the IS manager leads his or her organization into an architected environment, one of the considerations is the effect that architecture will have on the development process. Indeed, development does change in the face of architecture.

The first effect that architecture has on the development process is one that is apparent to the classical information systems development staff. Figure 4.15 shows this effect. The classical stance of the application developer is to gather a large amount of requirements (in fact, *all* the relevant requirements, if they can be found), bundle the requirements up, and create a design. Once the design is created, development ensues and a classical, legacy application implementation follows.

The classical development process is only slightly altered by going to the architected environment. While the application developer gathers up as many requirements as possible, those requirements are split into two distinct categories— operational requirements and informational requirements. Operational requirements continue to be developed in the

the classical design/development process

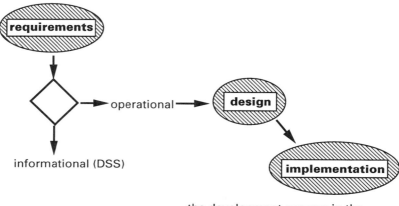

informational (DSS)

the development process in the
face of the information architecture

Figure 4.15.   The effect of architecture on the development process.

classical style. Informational requirements are sent to the data warehouse environment for inclusion there. The result is a much-streamlined development process.

The second effect of architecture on the development process occurs at the end-user environment. There, the question must be raised whether the processing that is done is of an operational nature. Figure 4.16 illustrates this analysis. If processing is of an operational nature, the processing must be sent to the operational environment. Otherwise, the processing can be done at the end-user level.

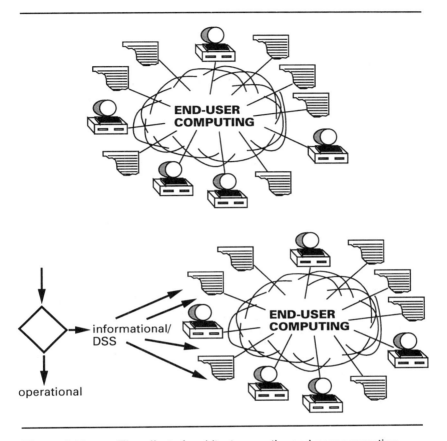

Figure 4.16.   The effect of architecture on the end-user computing environment.

Another consideration of the development process is data processing that is informational in nature. Figure 4.17 illustrates choices involved in informational processing. There are two kinds of informational processing that may be ferreted out from the legacy systems environment—ODS informational processing and data warehouse informational processing.

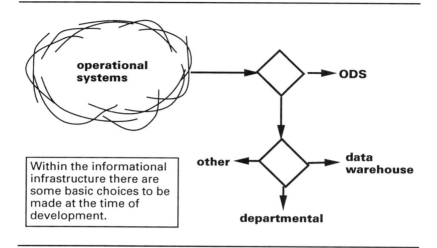

Within the informational infrastructure there are some basic choices to be made at the time of development.

Figure 4.17. Basic choices.

ARCHITECTURE AND REENGINEERING

There is a popular belief that techniques of reengineering should be applied to the production systems environment in order to resolve the many difficulties found there. Figure 4.18 shows that reengineering is a direction taken by many organizations for addressing the problems of legacy systems. Reengineering includes the techniques of data modeling, the application of CASE technology, the employment of business process reengineering, and so forth.

There is a very definite relationship between the success enjoyed in reengineering and architecture, although the relationship is hardly obvious. Simply stated,

> *in order to have a successful reengineering effort, you must first build the data warehouse and the information architecture.*

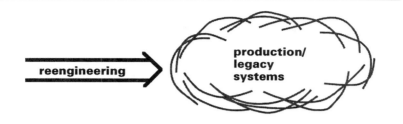

Figure 4.18.   Reengineering—an appealing approach.

The reverse is:

> *Trying to do reengineering without making data ware-house the first step is patently a mistake.*

Consider what happens to the production environment when the data warehouse is implemented. Figure 4.19 shows that when a company starts to build a data warehouse (or other parts of the informational architecture), there is a massive movement of data from the production environment into the data warehouse. Most of the data that is moved into the data warehouse is old, stale archival detail data that is seldom accessed. Yet that, stale data makes up a large percentage of the data found in the production environment. By moving stale data out of the production environment and into the data warehouse environment, the sheer volume of data in the production environment is reduced. It stands to reason that the reengineer facing the reengineering of 1gb of data is going to be much more successful and productive than the reengineer facing the restructuring and conversion of 100gb of data. So the first beneficial effect on reengineering of going to the data warehouse is the shrinkage of data in the production environment.

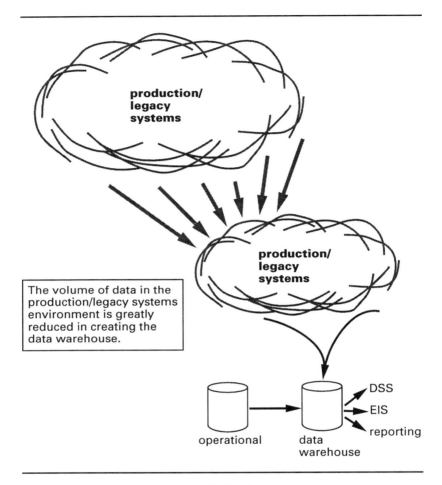

Figure 4.19. Reducing data with the data warehouse.

A second major beneficial effect of going to the data warehouse as the first step in reengineering is that of reshaping
the production workload, depicted in Figure 4.20.

In the production environment there is a lot of what can
be called "informational" processing. Informational processing occurs when a DSS analyst wants a report, or a new

informational processing:
  • reports
  • screens
  • sorts/merges
  • extracts
  • interfaces
  • spreadsheets, etc

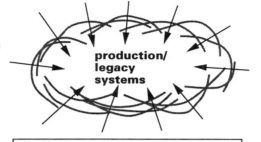

production/
legacy
systems

The production environment is filled
with informational processing because
that is the only place the DSS analyst
can do it.

Figure 4.20.   Where the processing is done.

screen, or an extract, and so forth. The DSS analyst has no
other place to turn to than the production environment in
order to do informational processing. The workload of the
production environment, then, is a hodge-podge of jobs,
many of which are informational in nature.

In order to understand the beneficial effect of going to
the data warehouse, consider the DSS analyst who is behind
the informational processing being done in the production
environment, as shown by Figure 4.21. The mindset of the
DSS analyst is "Give me what I say I want, then I can tell
you what I really want." In other words, the DSS analyst
operates in a state of discovery. Once the DSS analyst sees a
screen or a report, he or she understands what the possibilities are, and can refine the request for information.

This never-ending cycle of discovery and redefinition of
informational requirements soon leads to many requests for

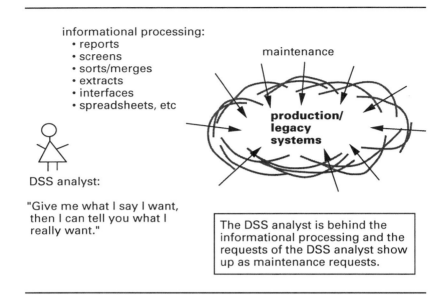

informational processing:
- reports
- screens
- sorts/merges
- extracts
- interfaces
- spreadsheets, etc

maintenance

production/
legacy
systems

DSS analyst:

"Give me what I say I want,
then I can tell you what I
really want."

The DSS analyst is behind the
informational processing and the
requests of the DSS analyst show
up as maintenance requests.

Figure 4.21.   The question of DSS analysis versus maintenance.

maintenance. The demand for informational processing in the production environment quickly turns into a stream of requests for maintenance in the production environment.

Worse, the faster the maintenance is accomplished, the faster the DSS analyst can change his or her mind and regenerate a new request for new production maintenance. The informational maintenance loop simply generates new maintenance requests as soon as one maintenance request is completed. In a sense, the maintenance for informational processing is "eternal" maintenance, because the cycle is never finished.

When the data warehouse is created, most of the informational processing moves to the data warehouse, as seen in Figure 4.22. Informational processing and the DSS analyst still operate in a cyclical fashion. But the regeneration of

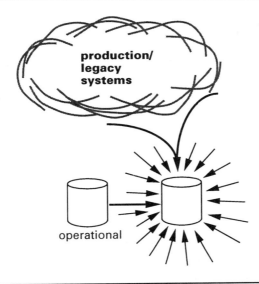

Figure 4.22. Moving informational processing to the data warehouse environment.

maintenance requests is done at the data warehouse, not the production environment. The net effect is that the production environment is greatly simplified and greatly streamlined by the removal of informational processing. Once the production environment is streamlined and simplified, the techniques of reengineering can start to be effective.

In short, when the data warehouse is the first step for reengineering:

- the production environment is greatly reduced, in terms of volume of data, and
- the workload of the production environment is greatly simplified and streamlined by the removal of informational requests.

The creation of the data warehouse and the establishment of the informational environment sets the stage for successful reengineering. As we have seen, not building the data warehouse as the first step in reengineering is patently a mistake.

EMPLOYING THE ENTERPRISE MODEL

A final use of the informational architecture is that of effective deployment of the enterprise data model. Figure 4.23 shows that the corporation has invested in the development of a corporate data model—an *enterprise data* model.

The usage of the enterprise data model varies according to the part of the architecture where the model is being considered. In other words, how the model is used is not the same for the legacy systems environment as it is for the end-user environment. The enterprise data model is used for the purposes of design and integration by the developer dealing with

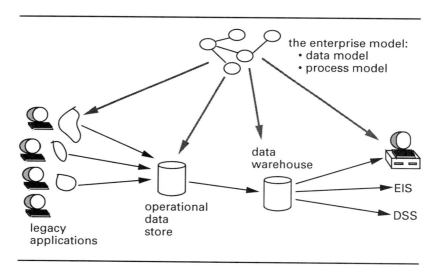

Figure 4.23. The reality of the enterprise model.

legacy systems. The enterprise data model is used directly in the design process for the building of the ODS and the data warehouse, and for the purpose of understanding what the possibilities for DSS processing are at the end-user level.

SUMMARY

The IS manager finds the notion of architecture indispensable in moving the corporation into a world of effective information processing. In particular, the IS manager uses architecture as a guideline for management of the following:

* storage use and acquisition,
* fitting technology with processing needs,
* managing the budget,
* managing and predicting growth,
* changing technologies and platforms,
* deriving information out of the production environment,
* determining organizational responsibilities,
* developing a reporting architecture,
* defining the interface between the different organizational units,
* managing the organization chart insofar as the responsibilities of information processing are concerned, and
* managing the impact of architecture on the development process.

In addition, architecture is the first step in the effective use of reengineering techniques.

5

Using the Data Warehouse: The End User's Perspective

Once the data warehouse is built and the first data is transformed and populated into the warehouse, it then falls to the end user—the DSS analyst—to unlock the secrets of information that are held within the bits and bytes of the warehouse. The objective of the end user is informational processing, and it is the data warehouse that is the enabler of informational processing.

WHO IS THE END USER?

The end user is someone who is first and foremost a businessperson and secondarily a technician, if a technician at all. The primary objective of the end user is to make the business run better. The business goals of the end user typically are:

- increasing market share,
- reducing costs and expenses, and
- increasing revenues.

To the end user, the data warehouse is merely a means to an end. The data warehouse is the vehicle by which the business runs efficiently and effectively. As a rule, the end user is in an advisory position to management. Only infrequently will the end user be in a position to directly interface with the customer or interact in the day-to-day activities of the corporation.

The focus of the end user doing analytical processing based on the data found in the warehouse is on long-term or medium-term business decisions. Only infrequently will the end user access a data warehouse for the purpose of an immediate business need. The ODS is the place to turn to when addressing immediate day-to-day needs. Strategy and tactics are the objective of gathering information out of the data warehouse, not operational, immediate decisions.

The Holy Grail for the end user is insight as to why business has been conducted the way it has been in the past and how business can be conducted more effectively in the future. Even one iota of insight of the proper type can pay off enormous benefits to the organization employing the data warehouse. In the final analysis, the informational processing done by the end user reaches the bottom line of the corporation in a very positive and noticeable way.

The end user typically is from the finance, marketing, or sales organization, although other departments are discovering the advantages of doing informational processing. Figure 5.1 shows the various types of end users.

As a rule, the closer informational processing is to the main line of the business of the corporation, the greater the chances of a significant payoff. Trying to do informational processing effectively in the outposts of the corporation is usually an exercise in futility. Even if the most beneficial informational processing is done in the backwaters of the company, there is little chance that the beneficial results will strongly or noticeably affect the bottom line of the corpo-

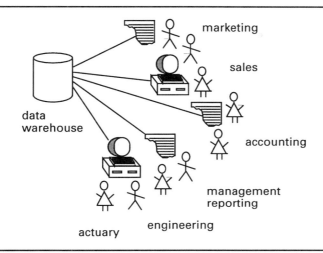

Figure 5.1.   The end users.

ration. Therefore, wherever the main line of operation of the company is, that is the place to start to employ informational processing.

If a company is primarily a manufacturer, then it makes sense to try to use informational processing to improve the efficiency and the effectiveness of the manufacturing process. If a company is a retailer, then it makes sense to use informational processing at the point where sales are being made. If a company is a service agency, then it makes sense to use informational processing at the point of the delivery of services.

CASUAL USERS/POWER USERS

There is a spectrum of users in the data warehouse/informational processing arena. Some end users make extensive use of the data warehouse; other end users make little use of informational processing. The spectrum of users is shown in

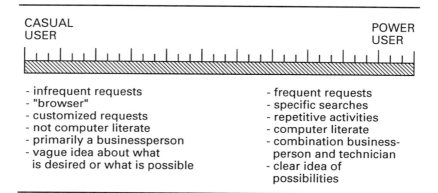

Figure 5.2. The end-user knowledge spectrum.

Figure 5.2. At one extreme are the power users. These are analysts who are computer literate, motivated, and have a clear idea of what they are looking for. The power user employs the data warehouse frequently. The data warehouse provides key information for making decisions. The power user regularly integrates information into the conduct of business. At the other end of the spectrum is the casual user, who rarely uses informational processing. The casual user is often computer illiterate, with only vague ideas about the possible uses of information in improving the decision-making process. In truth, most users are somewhere in the middle of the spectrum.

There is no question that the power user is the most important person to the corporation in regard to the establishment of the data warehouse and the unleashing of the power of informational processing. The more power users the corporation has, the greater the chance that information will be used effectively.

But the casual user is also important. In terms of unlocking latent informational processing, the casual user represents opportunity and potential. Interestingly, the casual user often makes accidental discoveries while using the data warehouse that are very important to the company. The casual user often has a different perspective, and this creates the potential for spawning innovative use of data and information.

INFORMATION AND THE ORGANIZATION

The end user can be at any level of the organization. The organization chart is spotted with end users throughout, as seen in Figure 5.3. The end user can be at the top of the organization chart or at the bottom. The forms of informational processing vary from one level of management to the next.

The type of informational processing at the top of the organization chart is typically EIS and key indicator analysis. Information at the top of the chart is usually very summary and strategic in nature. At the top of the organization chart the emphasis in informational processing is on long-term trends.

Informational processing in the middle of the organiza-

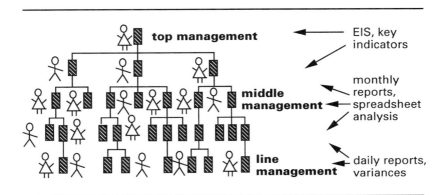

Figure 5.3.   User locations and needs.

tion chart is typically standard reports, spreadsheet analysis, and a wide variety of specialized informational processing. Indeed, informational processing usually has the greatest impact at the midlevel of the corporation. The emphasis on informational processing at the midlevel of the corporation is midterm information, from one week to one month old.

Informational processing at the bottom line of management of the corporation consists of very immediate and detailed variance analysis and daily reports. The emphasis of informational processing at the lower levels of the management of the corporation is on very immediate, short-term information.

At whatever level of the corporation and for whatever time horizon, having proper and accurate information means management is armed to make the best decisions possible.

THE WORLD OF THE END USER

The world of the end user who is doing informational processing is one of data, metadata, and tools for accessing information and creating analyses, as illustrated in Figure 5.4. The end user can be of two varieties—the direct user or the indirect user. The direct end user actually accesses the data warehouse directly. The indirect end user accesses a workstation or other processor. The workstation has previously accessed data from the data warehouse and has returned the data back to the workstation. (Note: The term "workstation" is used in the broadest context for the discussions in this book. A workstation may be something as small as a personal computer with Lotus 1-2-3 or something as large as a server with Oracle or Sybase.) Once the data has arrived at the workstation, the end user accesses and manipulates it there.

The end user—direct or indirect—has a host of tools that enable the effective use of his or her analytical environment.

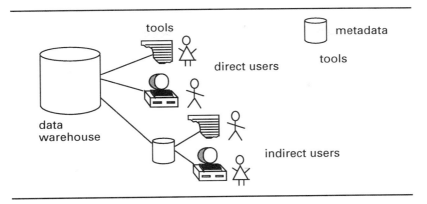

Figure 5.4.   The world as seen by the end user.

Some of the tools relate to the metadata. Others relate to the access and manipulation of the data itself. Reports can be generated. A single answer can be calculated. Spreadsheets can be created and manipulated. Graphs can be produced. There is no end to the ways data can be analyzed and presented by the available tools.

As a rule, when there is not much data in a data warehouse, or where there is summary data that is regularly calculated and regularly accessed, the data warehouse is accessed directly. But where there is much data in the data warehouse or where summary data is not calculated and stored on an ongoing basis, indirect usage of the data warehouse is the norm.

In addition, when there are special analyses that require much iterative processing, the data is lifted from the data warehouse, placed on a workstation, and indirect analysis is done.

The end user sees very little of the actual infrastructure of the data warehouse. For example, the background processing of refreshment of data into the warehouse is not apparent to the end user at all.

THE END USER AND METADATA

One of the most important aspects of the end user's environment is that of metadata. *Metadata* is simply data about data. In its simplest form, metadata appears to be a catalog of the contents of the data warehouse.

The role of metadata is best understood in terms of what the end user's environment looks like in the absence of metadata. Consider a world where there is only the end user and raw data. Management calls the end user one day and requests a special analysis to be done. If the end-user analyst happens to know where the appropriate data is in the data warehouse, then there is no problem. But consider what happens when the request from management requires access and manipulation of parts of the data warehouse that the end-user analyst has no knowledge of. How is the end user to proceed?

Inevitably, the end-user analyst proceeds by trial and error in the search for the appropriate data in the data warehouse. In a word, the end user is in a reactive state. If the end user is lucky, he or she finds data useful to the analysis that management has requested. But precious time could be spent looking for what might not turn out to be the right data in the data warehouse.

Now consider the same scenario in the presence of metadata that is readily available to the end-user analyst. When management requests analysis from the end user and the end user is not familiar with the data that is required, it is metadata that allows the end user to peruse the possibilities for analysis. No trial-and-error searching for data in the data warehouse is necessary. The end user is in a proactive position to respond to management's requests in a positive and timely fashion. Metadata is like a roadmap for a journey into unfamiliar territory.

Figure 5.5 shows some of the types of metadata that

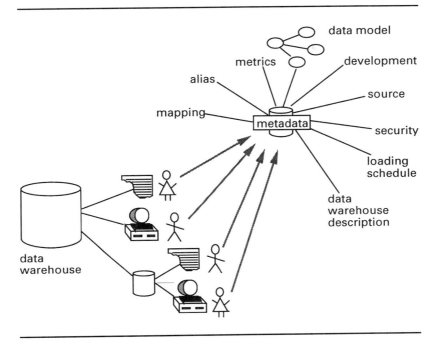

Figure 5.5. Metadata and the end user.

might be found in the end-user environment that the end-user analyst will be interested in. There is a wide variety of metadata that needs to be available to the end-user analyst. Some of these are listed here:

- *The source of the data in the data warehouse—the identi-fication of the "system of record":* Knowing what the original, unintegrated operational systems are for the tables in the data warehouse is useful when the very source of data for the warehouse is called into question.
- *The transformation that has occurred from the time the data resided in the unintegrated, operational environment until the data arrived in the data warehouse:* In

some cases, very little is done to the data as it passes into the warehouse; in other cases much processing is done. In order for the end user to understand what data really represents and what the best source for analysis in the data warehouse is, transformation data is needed.

- *The actual description of the data in the data warehouse:* This is the simplest of the metadata requirements. The end user needs to know what tables are available, what fields there are in the tables, the descriptive information about the fields, and the physical characteristics of the fields in order to formulate requests.

- *"Versioning" to the storage of the essential metadata over time:* From January to February there may be one source of data for a table, but in March the source may have changed. Since the data is stored in the data warehouse continuously, there is a need to keep track of metadata over time. In other words, in order to do effective analysis, the end user needs to know that at one point in time there was one source of data and at another point in time there was another source of data for the same table in the data warehouse.

While some aspects of metadata are mandatory, other aspects are not mandatory, but are nevertheless quite useful. Some of the optional forms of metadata include the following:

- *Metrics:* This refers to simple counts and profiles of data in the data warehouse. Metrics allow the end user to be alerted beforehand that a request may take a large amount of resources. If there is any doubt as to whether a request will access many records, a glance at the metrics tells the end user whether caution is in order.

- *Alias information:* Alias information allows a field to be called by more than one name. One department may know data in the data warehouse by one name and another department may call the same data something else. With alias information, the data warehouse is able to satisfy the needs of the different organizations that have different naming conventions and standards.

- *Data model information:* At the heart of the shaping of the data warehouse is the data model. The data model is useful to the end user analyst in that it provides a high-level roadmap for finding out what data is in the warehouse. The linkage between the data model and the tables of the data warehouse can be very important in the strategic usage of the data in the data warehouse.
- *Development:* The data warehouse is in a constant state of development. Keeping track of what has been implemented and what is in the works is important to the end-user analyst.
- *Security:* Data warehouse requires a more fundamental level of security than other forms of databases. The end-user analyst needs some indication of what data is protected and where to look if access to protected data is required.
- *Loading schedule:* While accessing data is important, the end user also needs to know when the data was last refreshed (last night, today, or last month?).

Another important dimension of metadata is that it may be local or global, as illustrated in Figure 5.6. *Global metadata* is metadata that applies for all the data warehouse. Any end user should have access to global metadata. Local metadata is data that applies only to a single end-user analyst or class of end-user analysts. Only certain analysts will have access to local metadata. Usually, global metadata is stored with the data warehouse itself. *Local metadata* usually applies to indirect usage of the data warehouse and resides on the workstation or in the immediate environment that is available to the workstation. Metadata, then, plays

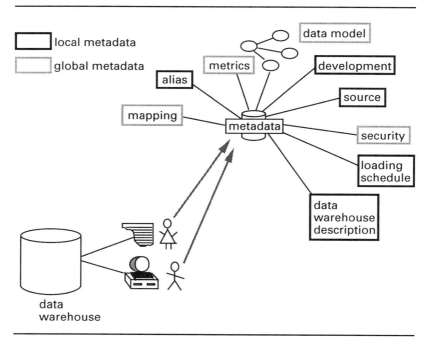

Figure 5.6.   Global and local metadata.

an important role in defining the environment of the end-user analyst.

QUERYING THE DATA WAREHOUSE

The end user accesses the data warehouse through what is termed a "query." A query is simply a request for access to information in the data warehouse, with possibly some processing of that data before the results of the query are returned to the end user. A query can take on many flavors and forms. In order to understand the access to the data warehouse that the end user enjoys, a taxonomy of queries is required.

Figure 5.7 shows some different aspects of queries. Some queries look at a lot of data; other queries look at only a record or two. In most cases, it is possible for the sophisticated end user to distinguish between the two types of queries before the query is submitted. Sometimes, however, even the most sophisticated end user cannot tell how many records a query will look at before the query goes into execution. It is important to know the number of records a query will look at prior to execution, because queries that access lots of records require special treatment.

A second aspect of queries is that some are submitted repeatedly and others are submitted only once. Queries that are repeatedly and predictably submitted have to have special care because they form the backbone of end-user analytical processing.

Another important characteristic of queries is that some

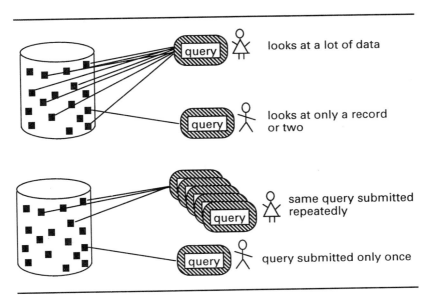

Figure 5.7.   The varieties of end-user queries.

are executed in an iterative (i.e., heuristic) fashion and some are executed in a "precanned" fashion, as illustrated in Figure 5.8.

Iterative analysis is the process of submitting a query, looking at the results, restating the query, and resubmitting it. In iterative processing, the next step of analysis cannot be known until the current step is completed and the results can be examined. In other words, the results of one step of processing suggest what the next step should be. The process of restatement and resubmission continues until the end user discovers what it is that is being searched for. (In some circles the end user is said to have this mindset: "I don't know what I am looking for, but when I find it I will know it.") Iterative analysis is a powerful method of discovery or exploration. In many ways, it makes the most of the data warehouse. The amount of records that are accessed by any given iteration is unknown. Sometimes a few records are accessed; other times many records are accessed.

At the other end of the spectrum is the execution of *precanned* queries. In this case, the end user knows exactly what is being sought. The query runs many times, reanalyz-

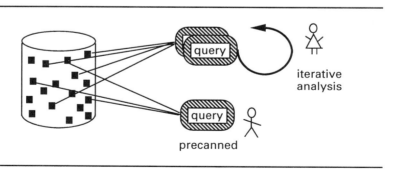

Figure 5.8.   Planned versus ad hoc queries.

ing the same data or looking at different data. Typically, precanned queries use a small number of records.

There is a very predictable path that an organization goes through in the creation of the well-established, precanned queries. Figure 5.9 shows that a query is first built as an iterative query. Several iterations ensue. But once these have been done, the query stabilizes. At this point, the query begins to be run frequently.

Of course, not all iterative analyses result in regularly scheduled queries. Some iterative analyses lead nowhere. Other iterative analyses are of a onetime variety and will never be run again.

An interesting question is who should be responsible for the creation of the syntax of the query. This issue is relevant for queries that will be run directly against the data warehouse.

A case can be made that the end user should be the person creating the syntax. The end user best knows his or her own needs. The end user is ultimately the person who will determine whether a query has been successful or not. And when a corporation has a chargeback system for paying for resources consumed, it is the end user that pays for the execution of the query. Adding any other person into the loop— the database administrator (DBA) or anyone else—simply

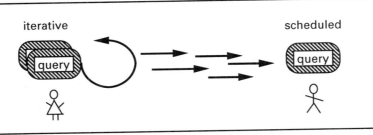

iterative   scheduled

Figure 5.9.   Predictability for scheduling iterative analysis.

creates another level of bureaucracy that stands in the way of progress. For these reasons (and many more) a strong case can be made for having the end user create and execute the syntax of the queries.

But there is also a valid case to be made for having the DBA or some other information systems professional actually create the syntax of the query. When the DBA creates the syntax of the query there is little chance that the query will consume an undue amount of resources. The DBA is computer literate and should not stumble over simple syntactical and technical errors. And the DBA has the perspective of the entire data warehouse in mind and may well spot an error of judgment before the query goes into execution.

Figure 5.10 illustrates the dilemma of who creates the syntax. Resolving this dilemma is a matter of judgment and management. The responsibilities should be divided according to the type of query. For queries that are repetitive, where a lot of data may be accessed, or where the requirement has been generated from a classical requirements analysis, the DBA is probably the best person to develop the syntax. For queries where there is a onetime execution of

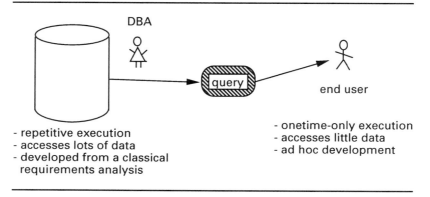

DBA

query

end user

- repetitive execution
- accesses lots of data
- developed from a classical
  requirements analysis

- onetime-only execution
- accesses little data
- ad hoc development

Figure 5.10.   Who should develop the query?

the query, where the query will access very little data, or where the development is being done on an ad hoc basis, the end user is best to develop the query. There is a gray area where it is unclear who should develop the syntax for the query. In these cases the best judgment should be made weighing all the factors.

Over time, the workload that operates against the data warehouse changes dramatically. Figure 5.11 typifies that change. In the very early days of the data warehouse almost all processing against the data warehouse is free-form, unstructured processing. Many joins are done, and there emerges no real pattern of processing. In addition, there is usually a plethora of machine resources that are available.

As time passes, the workload changes. There still is some amount of free-form, unstructured processing that occurs, but the workload soon becomes dominated by structured, tightly coded queries. Very little join activity occurs. At the same time, more and more machine resources are being used, so there are less free resources to go around.

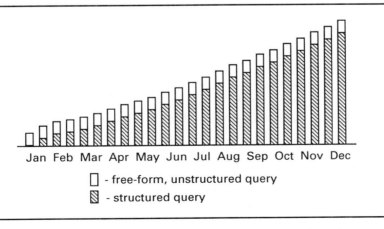

Figure 5.11.   The trend of structured versus unstructured queries.

EFFICIENCY OF ACCESS

There are two important reasons (among others) why the end user is interested in the speed of access and the efficiency of queries that operate directly on a data warehouse:

- The more efficiently a query runs, the less expensive the query is.
- The faster a query runs, the faster the end user can move through the iterative development process.

The last point bears close analysis. Consider an end user who submits a request that executes in twenty-four hours. Upon receiving the results of the query, the end user does analysis and reformulates the request. The request is then resubmitted. But a full day has passed since the original submission of the query. The lengthy time of execution impedes the iterative process.

Now consider another end user who is able to execute his or her request in ten minutes. Upon execution, the results of the request are analyzed. The request is reformulated and resubmitted. However, this end user is able to go through the entire iterative process in half a day because there is fast turnaround of processing. Simply by having much greater speed of execution, the second analyst is much more productive than the first.

There is, then, a very real, if indirect, relationship between the speed of execution of the end user's query and the productivity of the end user. A query that executes quickly facilitates the entire iterative process.

In many ways, the efficiency of a query's access to data and execution is determined at the moment of design. When a data warehouse is designed properly, access is natural and easy. When the data warehouse has not been designed properly, almost nothing the end user does is effective in speeding up the execution of the query. Notwithstanding the importance of proper design (which in the final analysis the end user has little say over), there still are some measures that the end user can take to enhance execution, as outlined in Figure 5.12.

The first step the end user can take toward good performance is to use indexes when accessing data. Using an index allows for only selected records to be accessed rather than for the access of massive amounts of records, most of which are not needed. This simple measure is quite effective and can cut down resource utilization enormously in the processing of a query. However, on occasion data must be accessed where there is no index. And in some cases there may well be an index on the data to be accessed but the DBMS managing the data warehouse is unable to take advantage of it.

A second step the end user can take to optimize query

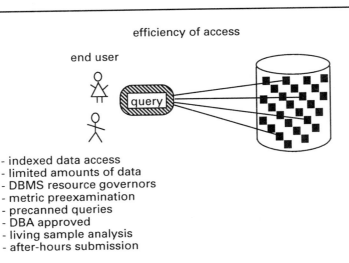

Figure 5.12.   Some techniques for end user access efficiency.

performance is to make sure that only the minimum amount of data need be accessed in order to satisfy the intent of the request. In some cases, merely limiting the amount of data accessed by a query has a beneficial effect on performance. In other cases, there is no effective way to limit the amount of data needed for a query.

A third technique the end user may occasionally take advantage of is that of halting the execution of a large query by means of a resource governor. Some DBMS have internal counts of resources that are made while the query is actually in execution. When a query exceeds the access of a predetermined number of resources, it is terminated. While the use of a resource governor prevents any resource hogs from being turned loose on the data warehouse, this approach is crude. The problem is, what action does the system take upon termination of the query? In short, there is no good or elegant answer.

A fourth technique for the management of the resources consumed by a query is that of metric analysis prior to submission. Metrics about the contents of the data warehouse may exist. When metrics exist, the end user is able to see whether the request submitted will be operating on a large or a small database. If the query is to run against a large database, the end user may want to rephrase or otherwise repackage the request.

A fifth approach to the management of query resource utilization is to use only precanned queries. By using precanned queries, the end-user analyst is assured that the query has been optimized and debugged.

A sixth approach is to engage the services of the DBA prior to the submission of any new query. The DBA or any other qualified technical personnel looks over the request to see if there are any red flags. The difficulty with this approach is that it destroys the spontaneity of iterative analysis and introduces an element of bureaucracy that otherwise would not be present.

A seventh approach is to do what is called "living sample" analysis. (Note: Living sample analysis is discussed in ample measure in the References at the back of this book.) Living sample analysis requires that the first few iterations of analysis be done against a small subset of data. Only when the request has been completely formulated is the request run against the full body of data.

A final approach is to submit large, bulky jobs only in the after-hours of processing, when the machine is otherwise unoccupied. Even though a query may be very large, it can at least be run so that it has minimal impact on other processing in the data warehouse.

While all of the above approaches apply when the query must be run directly against the data warehouse, there is an alternative approach, where the data can be taken from the data warehouse on a onetime basis and shipped to another platform. Once the data has been shipped to another platform, the end user analyzes the data with no thought of resources consumption at the data warehouse. Figure 5.13 displays this technique.

The alternate platform that holds the extracted data can be called a "departmental processor." Once the data is sent to the departmental processor and queries and analysis are run against the departmental database, there obviously is no performance impact or consideration for the size of queries being run against the data warehouse. Large amounts of both data and processing are lifted out of harm's way.

An additional convenience is that the departmental processor can be customized for the needs of the end user. The end user has total control of the design and operations occurring in the departmental processor. Also, because the departmental processor is most likely much smaller than the

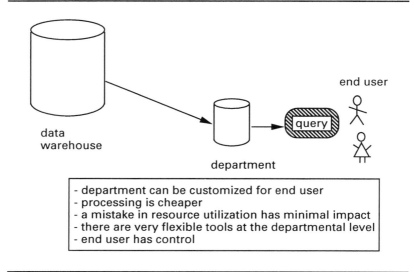

Figure 5.13. Moving query processing out to the departmental level.

processor running the data warehouse, processing on the departmental processor is usually significantly less expensive. The end user's iterative analysis costs much less to run on the departmental machine than the same processing would on the data warehouse machine. If there are any mistakes in judgment as to resource utilization on the departmental machine, the results are unnoticed in the data warehouse machine. A final reason why moving data warehouse data down to the departmental level is so popular is that there often exist very powerful analytical tools at the departmental level that do not exist at the data warehouse level.

For all the advantages of doing end-user processing on a departmental machine there are some disadvantages. If the initial load of data from the data warehouse machine to the departmental machine does not include all the data that is necessary for the end user's analysis, then there may well be a later disruption at the data warehouse level to reintroduce more data. For this reason, more than enough data is included in the initial pass of loading the departmental database. Another difficulty is that the data in the departmental processor is only as fresh as the moment when it was initially loaded. The departmental processor is normally not constantly refreshed. Departmental data ages rapidly. This lack of currency may or may not pose a problem to the end-user analyst.

MANAGING REALLY LARGE QUERIES

Even in the best of circumstances, occasionally the end user will be faced with the problem of having to execute a really large request. Figure 5.14 illustrates the options the end user has in this case.

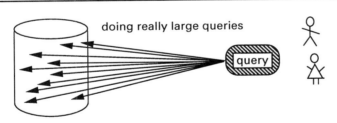

doing really large queries

query

- break query into subsets
  - by query function
  - by data
- run after hours
- move data to other processor
- prepackage the data
- checkpoint processing
- use living sample techniques

Figure 5.14.   Some techniques for managing queries that access very large amounts of data.

If a query is going to be really large, the end-user analyst can do any of the following:

- Break the request into a series of smaller requests. As a rule, there are many ways to make this break—by query function, by divisions of data, by geography, by time, etc.
- Run the request after hours, when the full resources of the machine can be dedicated to smooth and efficient running.
- Move the data to another processor and execute there.
- Prepackage the data so that it is efficient to execute against.
- Checkpoint the query so that if need be it can be broken into a series of smaller requests.
- Use living sample techniques, if possible.

CHANGING GRANULARITY

Whether the problem is massive volumes of data or the amount of processing against that data, there is always a general technique that can be applied. That technique is called the changing of the granularity of data, as seen in Figure 5.15. (The topic of granularity of data has been discussed in many books and articles and will not be repeated here. Instead the discussion will address only the focal points.)

Granularity of data refers to the level of detail of the data in the data warehouse. Very granular data warehouse data necessarily entails much volume and much detail. Very coarse data warehouse data entails less detail and far fewer occurrences of units of data. One way to grossly reduce the amount of data processed against in a data warehouse is to raise the granularity of data. The raising of the level of granularity always reduces the amount of data and processing required in the use of the data warehouse—in most cases very dramatically.

But there is a tradeoff. By raising the level of granular-

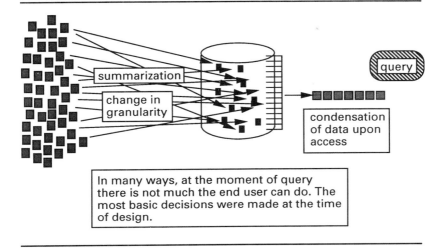

In many ways, at the moment of query
there is not much the end user can do. The
most basic decisions were made at the time
of design.

Figure 5.15.   Managing large volumes of data.

ity of data in the data warehouse, the data becomes limited
in scope in terms of what kind of analysis the data in the
warehouse can be used for.

As an example of the potency of changing the level of
granularity, consider an example. The same analytical results can be achieved from the analysis of different levels of
granularity of data found in a data warehouse, but very different amounts of data need to be accessed, as seen in Figure 5.16, where two queries are submitted that functionally
accomplish exactly the same thing. The only difference between the queries is that they are going against data that is
at different levels of granularity. Many processing resources
are required when the detail of phone calls made are accessed. Fewer resources are required when the same request
is made of data that is summarized by customer by month
than if the same request were run against detailed data.
Simply by changing the level of granularity, the end-user
analyst has created the same analysis at very different costs.

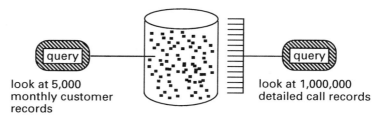

"How many long distance phone calls did customers in area code 303 make last month?"

query

look at 5,000 monthly customer records

query

look at 1,000,000 detailed call records

> The level of detail at which a query is issued makes a huge difference in how many resources are used—the end user should be conditioned to submit queries at the highest level of granularity.

Figure 5.16. An example of the highest level of granularity.

UPON EXECUTION ...

Once the query is executed there may be several dispositions of the results of the query, as shown in Figure 5.17. A wide variety of dispositions may occur, because they depend on a variety of factors, such as the end user, the type of analysis the end user is doing, the data generated by the analysis, further iterative analysis that might be done, and so forth. The possibilities for disposition include the following:

- the delivery of a simple statement—a one-line answer that is needed by the end user,
- the delivery of a formal report that the end user takes in as part of the business process,
- the creation of a new set of data, refined and culled from the data warehouse,

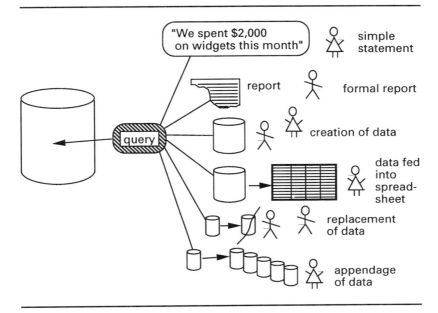

Figure 5.17.   What happens to a query once it is executed.

- the creation of a set of data that is then fed into further analysis, such as a spreadsheet,
- the creation of a set of data that then replaces a previously generated set of data, and
- the appendage of the newly created set of data onto a like set of previously created data.

FRONT-END QUERY CREATION

How exactly does the end user create the request for the data warehouse? A typical way the request is created is through front-end workstation editing. Figure 5.18 illustrates a front-end edit.

At the workstation the end user accesses a query generation tool (such as Brio). The front-end query generation (feqg)

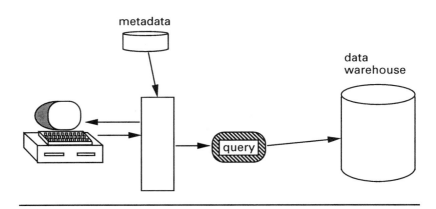

Figure 5.18.   Front-end query creation/direct end-user interface.

tool has access to metadata. The metadata is displayed to the end user, usually in table form. The end user then browses through the possibilities for access, and selects tables, or fields from tables for access. If there is a need for a join (or joins), the back-end query generation tool edits the request to see if a join is possible. In addition, other metadata may be available to help the end user select the appropriate data for selection. Meta-information such as alias information, metric information, and indexing are available to help the end user refine the existing choices.

Once the end user has specified what the query is to be, the front-end query generator the turns the request into code that is intelligible to the DBMS managing the data warehouse, typically SQL.

The sequence of events might occur in this way:

```
10:01 am (end-user analyst) - "What tables are
                              available for me to look
                              at in the data
                              warehouse?"
```

```
10:02 am (feqg) - "You can look at the following
                    tables - "
                 acctspay
                 acctsrec
                 acctsovd
                 acctchar
                 acctactv
                 acctinac
                 activ911
                 activ912
                 activ913
                 ........
10:07 am (end-user analyst) - "This table acctactv
                                looks interesting. What
                                is the description of
                                acctactv?"
10:08 am (feqg) - "The description is - "
        acctactv - all active accts as of year start
10:10 am (end-user analyst) - "What fields are there in
                                acctactv?"
10:11 am (feqg) - "The fields for acctactv are - "
        acctnumb
        acctname
        acctaddr
        acctfdat
        acctdomi
        accttype
        acctlmtl
10:12 am (end-user analyst) - "What descriptions are
                               there for the fields
                               found in acctactv?"
10:13 am (feqg) - "The fields are described as - "
        acctnumb - account number
        acctname - name assigned to the account
        acctaddr - address of the account
        acctfdat - date account first opened
        acctdomi - account domicile
        accttype - type of account
        acctlmtl - account credit card limit
10:14 am - (end-user analyst) - "What's the key for
                                  acctactv?"
```

```
10:15 am - (feqg) - "The key for acctactv is - "
             acctnumb
10:16 am - (end-user analyst) - "What do the physical
                                 characteristics of
                                 acctactv look like?"
10:17 am - (feqg) - "The physical characteristics are - "
       acctnumb     char(16)
       acctname     varchar(25)
       acctaddr     varchar(25)
       acctfdat     char(6)
       acctdomi     pic 9
       accttype     char(1)
       acctlmt1     dec fixed(15,2)
10:20 am - (end-user analyst) - "How many occurrences
                                 of acctactv are
                                 there?"
10:21 am - (feqg) - "The number of occurrences of
                     acctactv as of Sept 15 are - "
             17,992
10:25 am - (end-user analyst) - "Is the field acctnumb
                                 found anywhere else as
                                 a key?"
10:26 am - (feqg) - "The field acctnumb is found as a
                     key in the following tables - "
       acctspay
       acctsrec
       acctsovd
       acctinac
       custrec1
       ........
10:27 am (end-user analyst) - "Join the tables acctactv
                                 and acctchar on
                                 acctnumb"
10:28 am - (feqg) - "The resultant joined table looks
                     like - "
       acctnumb
       acctname
       acctaddr
       acctfdat
       acctdomi
       accttype
```

```
           acctlmt1
           chardesc
           chartype
           charclas
10:30 am - (end-user analyst) - "For the joined tables
                                 acctactv and acctchar
                                 search for all
                                 acctnumb from 10000 to
                                 20000 and acctchar
                                 equal "petcash""
10:31 am - (feqg) - "Request is complete, do you want
                     to issue?"
10:32 am - (end-user analyst) "Please show me the SQL
                               before issuing request"
10:33 am - (feqg) "The SQL request looks like - "
           SELECT acctnumb acctname acctaddr acctfdat
                  acctdomi accttype acctlmt1 chardesc
                  chartype charclas
           FROM acctactv, acctchar
           WHERE acctactv.acctnumb = acctchar.acctnumb AND
                 acctnumb BETWEEN 10000 AND 20000 AND
                 acctchar = "petcash"
......
......
......
```

Now that the query request has been formatted and has been examined by the end-user analyst, it is ready for submission.

A variation of the query is the *triggered query*. The triggered query is illustrated by Figure 5.19, where a query sits in a permanent position at the platform where the data warehouse is housed. As activities are run against the data warehouse, the triggered query monitors the data residing in the warehouse. Once the condition that the triggered query is waiting for exists, a response is sent to the user.

In such a manner the data warehouse becomes proactive, at least from the perspective of the end user. Without a trig-

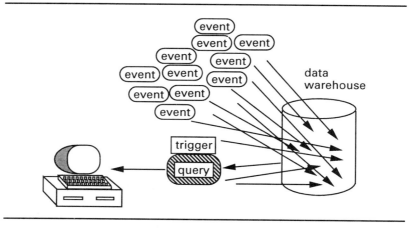

Figure 5.19.   A sophisticated trigger query.

gered query the data warehouse is essentially a passive construct.

One of the issues of the triggered query is the resources required for its ongoing monitoring. If the end-user analyst is not careful in the initial specification of the triggered query, a huge amount of resources can be consumed in the monitoring of the data warehouse and the activities that flow through the platform in its normal course of operation.

Another variation of the standard query is the composite query, illustrated in Figure 5.20. The composite query is one that is made up of multiple end-user queries. The composite query operates against a single table. The advantage of the composite query is that it combines the requirements for many queries into a single query. The result is that a single massive pass is made against the table being searched. Although the single massive search is expensive in terms of resource consumption, it is less expensive than if each of the individual queries made their own search for the data.

One limitation of the composite query approach is that it

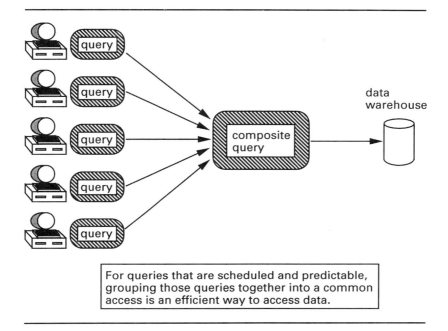

For queries that are scheduled and predictable, grouping those queries together into a common access is an efficient way to access data.

Figure 5.20.   Grouping scheduled and predictable queries.

is valid only for queries that can be run predictably, such as on a daily basis, and where the end user can afford to wait until the composite is executed. Unfortunately, many kinds of queries do not fit these criteria. But when a shop has queries that do fit the criteria, a composite query makes sense.

TRAINING THE END USER

There are many approaches to the training of the end user. Two of them will be discussed here.

Figure 5.21 shows the *power user approach* to training the end user in the possibilities of the data warehouse. In the early days of training, five or six power analysts are selected from the end-user community. These analysts are

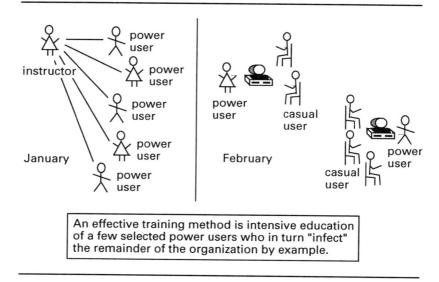

An effective training method is intensive education of a few selected power users who in turn "infect" the remainder of the organization by example.

Figure 5.21. The power user approach to training.

selected not for their technical prowess, but for their leadership and communication skills. These analysts are then instructed on a personal basis by the data architect managing the data warehouse effort. The training is not done in a formal manner. Instead the data architect sits down with the power user and personally teaches the end user everything he or she needs to know to become self-sufficient and effective. The topics covered include at least the following:

- how to log on to the workstation,
- how to hook into the data warehouse,
- how to find out what is in the data warehouse,
- how to create a query,
- how to issue a query,
- what the results of the query look like,

- why resource utilization is important,
- what the data model is,
- the mechanics of how the data warehouse works,
- where the data in the warehouse comes from,
- what mapping and transformation are,
- how to interpret the results of a query,
- how to save the results of a query, and
- how to store data as the result of a query.

After training, the power user returns to the operational community. Once returned to his or her job, the power user then begins to "infect" the other users. Other users view the possibilities and begin to explore the data warehouse on their own. In such a manner, the whole organization learns about the data warehouse.

The *standard approach* to end-user training is that of more traditional classroom courses. Figure 5.22 illustrates the classical approach to education, where courses are given to users in a standard setting. The curriculum follows the one prescribed

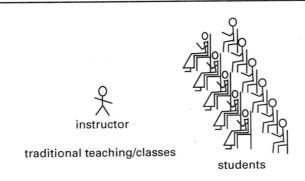

instructor

traditional teaching/classes

students

Figure 5.22.   The standard approach to training.

previously. The difference is that students are in a classroom environment rather than a one-on-one environment.

The standard approach to end user education is best where there are many end users that have to be educated all at once. The difficulty with mass education is that upon returning to the office environment, the end user will suffer a loss of continuity. After the education, the end user just does not know where to get started.

STEP BY STEP

If one were to draw a template for the end user in the classical usage of a data warehouse it would look like the steps outlined in Figure 5.23.

The first step in using the data warehouse is to decide that there is a need for information. This early analysis step attempts to pin down what kind of information is needed and where the data needed to support the information might be found.

Next, the analysis shifts to a search of the metadata. Metadata helps to delineate what the possibilities are. After the appropriate data is selected based on a search of the metadata, the request is shifted to the workstation level. At the workstation level the back-end query generator is enlisted. Then the request is generated.

After the request is generated, an analysis is made as to whether the request will consume an undue amount of resources.

The query is then submitted. The end user waits while the computer executes the query. Soon the results of the query are returned to the end user. An analysis of the results follows. Based on the results that have been achieved, either the analysis is over, or the request is modified and the process is begun again.

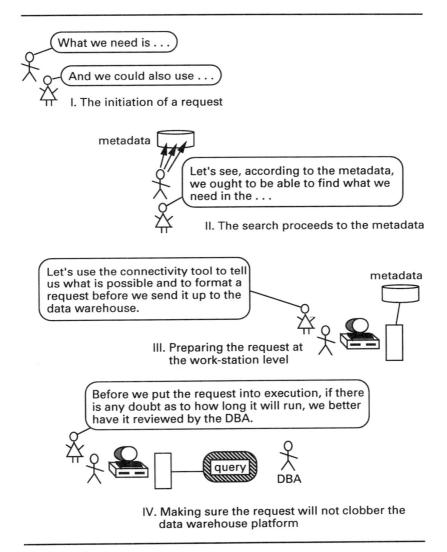

I. The initiation of a request

II. The search proceeds to the metadata

III. Preparing the request at the work-station level

IV. Making sure the request will not clobber the data warehouse platform

Figure 5.23.   Using the data warehouse. (*continued*)

Figure 5.23. *Continued*

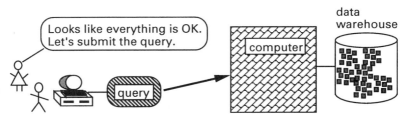

V. The query is submitted

VI. The query goes into execution

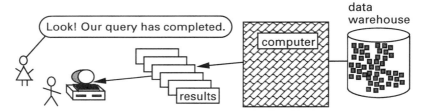

VII. The results of the query are returned

VIII. Analysis of the results

SUMMARY

The end-user analyst is typically from the marketing, sales, or finance departments. Some companies have users from other departments such as engineering or actuary. The closer informational processing is to the main line of business of the corporation, the greater the chance for effective informational processing. Users can be rated on a scale of casual user to power user.

The end user is found up and down the management chart. The end user sees a world of tools, metadata, and data from the warehouse. Metadata allows the end user to be proactive in the use of the data warehouse.

Query management is an important aspect of the end-user environment. Some end users query a lot of data; some query very little data. Some end users submit the same query repeatedly; other end users submit a query only once. Metadata can be divided into two classes—local metadata and global metadata.

The analysis done by the end user can be repetitive or iterative. In any case, there needs to be constant attention to the resources consumed by a query. The efficiency of access is important to both the community of end users who share common resources and the lone end user executing the individual query.

6

Using the Data Warehouse: Creating the Analysis

The usage of the data warehouse occurs from the perspective of the end-user analyst. As we saw in Chapter 5, the end-user analyst (the "DSS analyst") is primarily a businessperson, and secondarily a technician. The primary concern of the DSS analyst is the health and welfare of the business. The DSS analyst thinks in terms of such things as market share, profitability, competition, expenses, and production efficiency and quality. Only incidentally does the DSS analyst think in terms of technology. The data warehouse and its surrounding analytical environment are merely a means to an end.

The DSS analyst may choose to look at the data warehouse in either an off-hand, casual manner or in an analytical manner, methodically searching out the answers being sought. Both approaches (and all variations in between) are effective and in the right circumstances, absolutely appropriate.

The primary goal of the DSS analyst is to provide management with new information or different interpretations of old information with which to make better decisions. In many cases, the information provided by the information analyst reflects a perspective of information that has previously gone unnoticed. It is this change in perspectives that management finds so valuable in the decision-making process.

Typical DSS analysis might ask the following questions:

- "What region is making more sales per customer contact than other regions?"
- "What product has the slowest turnover? the slowest turnover in the summer? in the winter?"
- "How has the introduction of a new product differed in terms of market acceptance from other newly introduced products?"
- "How many hours of manpower production are required for one product versus another, similar product?"
- "How have the demographics of the customer base changed?"
- "Is there a correlation between the sales of my sales force and the amount of time they have spent being trained?"
- "Is there a correlation between the color in which a product is being manufactured in and the rate of sales?"

Analysis can be done on either the data warehouse or the operational data store (ODS).

There is a difference in the types of analysis that are accomplished on the data warehouse and on the ODS. The data warehouse is used for perspectives that lead to long-term decisions primarily the domain and responsibility of management. The ODS is used for short-term decisions that can be typified as executive operational decisions, even though the decisions may be corporate in nature and are made at the executive level. Just because a decision is made at the executive level does not mean that it is not operational. It is understood that summary or otherwise analyzed data in the data warehouse is data that, once calculated, can be stored and reused in the data warehouse. Conversely, summarizations and calculations made from the ODS are normally not stored or reused on a widespread basis.

In order to understand how analysis is done in the data warehouse environment, consider the perspective of the end-user analyst—the DSS analyst. Figure 6.1 shows the world of the DSS analyst. There are four important components in the world of the DSS analyst: the challenge presented by management, metadata that describes what the contents of the data warehouse are, the query tool used to formulate, package and execute the query, and the data warehouse itself.

Figure 6.1 shows that the challenge for information comes to the DSS analyst from management. In some cases, the parameters are well defined. Management knows what it wants and can articulate what the requirements are. Much more common is the case when management has a feeling that something is not quite right, and it is up to the DSS analyst to interpret management's concerns into concrete business terms. This "normal" case makes use of the technique of iterative processing. First, the DSS analyst hypothesizes one set of variables as being relevant to the problems of management and organizes and analyzes those variables. Feedback is given and the hypothesis is restated. The process of iterative analysis continues until management and the DSS analyst are satisfied that the vague reasons for uneasiness are well defined and quantified. Management may still end up with a feeling of uneasiness at the end of an iterative analysis, but at least they will have a much clearer idea of *why* they are uneasy.

Another usage of the data warehouse comes up when the DSS analyst browses the data warehouse, not looking for anything in particular. In this case, the DSS analyst covers much ground and stops to investigate further only when something unusual is encountered. Once something unusual is encountered, an iterative investigation ensues if warranted.

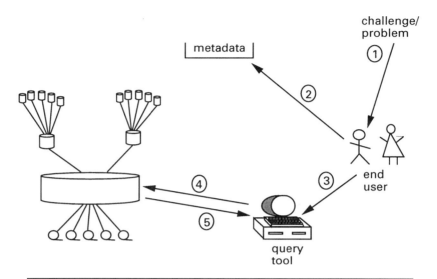

challenge/
problem

metadata

end
user

query
tool

Steps in creating the analysis:
1. Recognize that there is a problem or challenge.
2. Research the metadata in order to determine the plan of attack.
3. Formulate the query.
4. Submit the query.
5. Examine the results of the query.

Figure 6.1.   Creating the analysis.

Figure 6.2 shows that there is a broad spectrum of known requirements when the DSS analyst sets out to create an analysis. In some cases, the requirements are clear at the outset. In other cases, the parameters of the problem are not well understood.

Once the scope of the problems is understood (or at least estimated), the next step the DSS analyst takes in the analysis is to look at the metadata in order to determine the best line of attack in order to achieve analysis. Figure 6.1 illustrates the role of metadata.

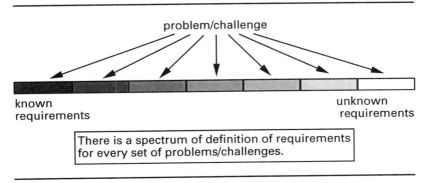

Figure 6.2.   The spectrum of definition of requirements.

The DSS analyst looks at metadata to determine

- what the most relevant data in the data warehouse is,
- the volume of data warehouse data that must be analyzed,
- the transformation of data in the data warehouse that has been done in order to bring the data into the warehouse,
- the originating source of the data, and so forth.

The DSS analyst searches the metadata to find the best source of data for the analysis at hand. The "heritage" of the data in the warehouse becomes of extreme interest, as the background of the data warehouse data greatly influences the usability and relevance of the data .

In addition to the heritage of the data in the data warehouse, the volume of data is of interest to the DSS analyst in creating the analysis. If a very large volume of data is going to be encountered, it is best to create the first of the analysis so that only a subset of data will be analyzed. This technique of operating in subsets is especially appropriate in the face of iterative analysis. It simply does not make sense to look at massive amounts of processing of data when the parameters of the query are still being formulated.

Another aspect of the formulation of the query is that of the timeliness of the data. If the data warehouse data is stored in monthly summarizations and the DSS analyst requires an analysis of daily totals, then the metadata tells the DSS analyst to look to another source of data for the analysis.

Once the DSS analyst has a notion of the statement of the problem and has examined metadata for the best fit between the problem and the data that resides in the data warehouse, the next task is to try to formulate the query into a format and structure acceptable to the query tool, as shown in Figure 6.1. In truth, many queries may be formulated as part of a single analysis. Also, it is highly unlikely that the DSS analyst will formulate any query correctly the first time around. If the DSS analyst does not have a technical bent, then he or she may want to enlist the aid of a technician at this point. If the query tool is user-friendly, or if the DSS analyst does have a technical background, then it may not be necessary to use the services of a technician for interfacing with the query tool.

Once the query has been created, the next step is to execute the query. The DSS analyst is not active during this part of the analytical process.

Once the query has been issued and returned, the DSS analyst then starts the interpretation of the results of the query. The first thing the DSS analyst asks is whether the query has been executed properly. If there has been a technical problem in the execution of the query, the analyst effects a cure and resubmits the query. Assuming the query has been technologically executed properly, the DSS analyst next asks whether the data that has been queried in fact was the right data. In some cases, the query may have executed on data other than what the analyst thought the query was to have executed on. In other cases, much more data was included than the DSS analyst realized; in yet other cases less data was examined. In any case, once the technical aspects of the query have been set in order, the DSS analyst needs to insure that the data that was intended for examination was in fact the correct data.

Once the DSS analyst has made these preliminary examinations, then the DSS analyst needs to interpret the results of the query. The interpretation of the results of the query requires a combination of intuition, business acumen, and technical knowledge. In some cases, the results will be surprising. The analyst must determine *why* the results are surprising. In many cases, in order to explain the results, another query will be run that explores more deeply other dimensions of the analysis. Sometimes, the DSS analyst must look to the technician for help in interpreting what the specification for the query really was. In other cases, the DSS analyst must turn to the businessperson to interpret the results.

GATHERING REQUIREMENTS

One of the interesting questions that face the DSS analyst is how much of the requirements for the analysis need to be known before the analysis commences. In some cases—such as in accounting and marketing systems—many of the requirements for analysis can be anticipated prior to the building of the analysis itself. In other cases—where browsing is the starting point—few requirements can be anticipated. There is a fine line to be walked in the gathering of requirements preceding the analysis. As a rule, the DSS analyst should gather all requirements that are obvious and easy to get. Any other requirements for the analysis most likely will not be gathered as a part of the analytical process. There is a good reason for this gathering of only easy-to-get requirements.

The process of gathering requirements can take an indefinite amount of time. A good consultant can gather requirements for as long as he or she is contracted, whether for a week or a month. With just a little creativity, a good consultant can find requirements almost indefinitely, especially when it comes to DSS, informational requirements. Furthermore, many of the obscure requirements are only tangentially helpful in creating the analysis the DSS analyst is interested in.

For these reasons, then, the DSS analyst is wise to "time box" the gathering of requirements. Figure 6.3 shows that the DSS analyst has gathered requirements that are obvious and easy to get. These requirements form the starting point for the analysis that is to ensue. Given that the analy-

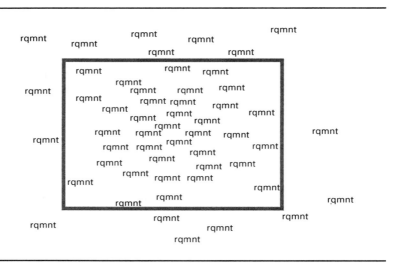

Figure 6.3. "Time boxing" the gathering of requirements.

sis will be done iteratively, other relevant requirements will surface if in fact they become important to the line of thought being engaged.

GETTING STARTED

One of the first questions the DSS analyst needs to ask is whether the analysis has a good chance of leading anywhere productive. While it is possible that informational process-ing can improve working and competitive conditions almost anywhere in the company, there are some classical places where informational processing has produced the quickest and most potent payback. When he or she "fishes in the right pond," the DSS analyst maximizes his or her chances of success. Figure 6.4 illustrates "fishing in the right pond."

The classical arenas that have produced the fastest and best results include

- finance,
- marketing,
- sales,
- actuary (for the insurance community),

fishing in the right pond:
- finance
- marketing
- sales
- actuary
- engineering
- customer profiling

Figure 6.4.   Making an "educated guess" as to where to start the DSS analysis.

- engineering (for the manufacturing community), and
- customer profiling.

There are several reasons why these arenas of activity are productive:

- They are near the main line of business of the organization. The closer the DSS analyst comes to creating a new perspective of information that relates to the heart of the business, the greater the chance that the DSS analyst will be listened to (and appreciated!).
- Management is always interested in money, and in particular the cash flow of the company. Any new insight into creating and managing a more effective cash flow of the organization always catches management's attention.
- In some cases (particularly finance), the amount of data that needs to be manipulated is finite and fairly disciplined. These factors make the data more malleable, which in turn leads to the ability of the DSS analyst to be able to analyze the data.

Analytical, informational processing can be used anywhere in the corporation. There are undoubtedly success stories that do not relate to the arenas that have been identified. Looking over the many success stories that have been generated by DSS analysts over the years, however, there starts to appear a pattern that suggests that there is an appropriate place for the DSS analyst to start.

USING THE METADATA

Once the requirements for the analysis have been gathered and assimilated (in whatever state of completeness they are in), the next step is to determine what data best serves the analyst's purpose. The organization's collection of metadata serves as the foundation for this analysis. Figure 6.5 shows the role of metadata.

Here are some of the questions the DSS analyst needs to ask as he or she searches through the metadata:

- What time frame is of relevance (only current valued data, data from a year ago, data from five years ago)?
- What subject areas are relevant to the analysis (sales, product manufacturing, customer buying patterns, vendor history)?
- What level of detail is required (very detailed, lightly summarized data, highly summarized data)?
- Can summaries of data over time be compared? Has the basis of the summary changed enough over time to warrant not comparing the data?
- How much data is going to be required—a small amount? So much that only representative sampling can be done?

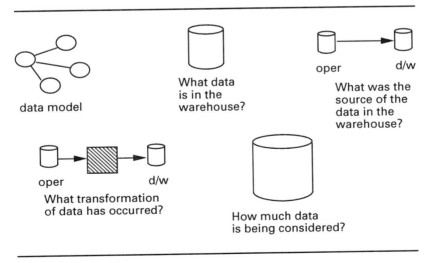

Figure 6.5.   Metadata helps to set the stage for the analysis.

- What exactly is the format and structure of the data in the data warehouse?
- What was the source of data in the operational environment—is the source appropriate? Is it the best source? Has the source changed over a long period of time?
- What transformation has been done to the data as it flowed from the source to the data warehouse? What conversions have been done? What reformatting and what filtering of data has been done?
- How does the data in the data warehouse relate to the enterprise data model? Is the data being analyzed the proper data? Is there a better source?

The metadata allows the DSS analyst to be proactive in the preparation of an analysis for management. Without metadata, the DSS analyst would have to discover these aspects of the data warehouse by trial and error.

FORMULATING THE QUERY

Once the DSS analyst has decided on the data that is to be queried, the next step is to formulate the actual request. Figure 6.6 depicts the formulation of the query.

The query can take many forms. It can be as simple as the submission of a single request for data. It can take the form of a request for a report. Or the query can take the form of a series of interrelated queries.

Exactly how the query is formulated is a function of the tools that the DSS analyst has at his or her disposal. Some query formulation tools are designed for a very smooth interface, where the DSS analyst is assumed to have little technical background. Other query tools are designed for the computer-literate DSS analyst. In this case the analyst merely creates the code that is needed.

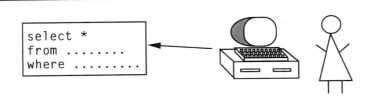

Figure 6.6.   Formulating the query.

An example of the user-friendly tools is Brio's Data
Prism. Brio's Data Prism allows the DSS analyst to first go
into the metadata and see what data is available for analysis. The DSS analyst picks out what data is of interest. Then
Data Prism determines if there is a need to merge data together from different sources in the data warehouse (commonly called a "join"). After the DSS analyst has specified
what data is needed and how it is related, Data Prism then
creates in the background the code necessary to access the
data and present it to the DSS analyst. Of course, the analyst can examine the code before it is sent to the data warehouse, but there is nothing that mandates that the code be
examined. However it is that the DSS analyst initiates the
analysis, the query tool is activated and the query is forwarded to the processor that manages the data warehouse.

INTERPRETING THE RESULTS

Once the results of the query are returned to the DSS analyst, it is then the job of the DSS analyst to interpret them.
Figure 6.7 shows this activity.

There are many different kinds of queries that can be
sent to the data warehouse. The simplest type of query is a
request for data, as shown in Figure 6.8. Here, the DSS

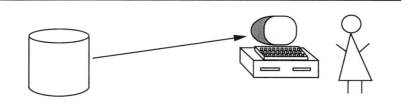

Figure 6.7. Interpreting the results.

analyst is simply looking up the status of a part as of a prior date. There is very little advance planning needed for this type of analysis.

A more sophisticated type of query is that of looking for trends. Figure 6.9 illustrates a query that looks for trends. The DSS analyst is trying to determine what the dropout rate has been over a lengthy period of time.

While trend analysis is a powerful way to approach informational processing, there are some basic problems that the DSS analyst should be aware of:

• Have the semantics of the data changed at the detail level over the period of trend analysis? If so, the trend analysis may lead to erroneous conclusions.

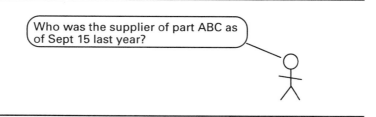

Who was the supplier of part ABC as of Sept 15 last year?

Figure 6.8. Looking for a single piece of information.

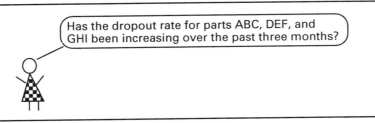

Figure 6.9. Identifying a trend.

- What conclusions can be drawn as a result of the analysis? Just because a trend has been identified does not necessarily mean that the cause of the trend is apparent. Incorrectly drawing conclusions as to the cause of a trend is a common fault in trend analysis.
- Is the trend statistically meaningful? Given a small enough sample size of data, all sorts of trends can be spotted that in reality are nothing more than truly random events. Drawing conclusions from random events is a very poor idea.

Browsing data is also a good way to initiate the analytical process. In Figure 6.10, the DSS analyst doesn't really know what he or she is looking for, but knows that when

Figure 6.10. Browsing data.

something of interest crosses his or her path, it will be apparent. Browsing data is a good practice. It is especially effective in the light of large amounts of data. In truth, browsing of data is the starting point for a deeper analysis.

Another form of analysis the DSS analyst engages in is that of doing comparisons. Figure 6.11 shows that the DSS analyst is comparing the sales of one product line to another. Management often finds these comparisons to be of interest. A word of caution is in order, however. When comparing any two things, there is the danger that apples will be compared to oranges. The factors that are relevant to one product line may be very different from the factors relevant to another product line. As long as it is understood that there is the danger of mixed comparisons, then the analysis shown in Figure 6.11 can be quite useful.

Combining comparisons with trend analysis results in an analysis that can be quite interesting, as depicted in Figure 6.12.

The contrast between the different trends allows management to view, in a quantified fashion, the comparative difference in results. While a set of comparisons over time can be quite interesting to management, such a comparison is subject to the different variables that are relevant to *both*

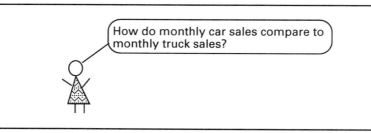

Figure 6.11.   Doing comparisons.

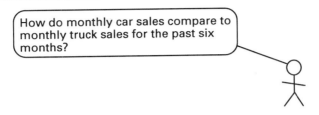

Figure 6.12.   Doing comparisons over time.

comparisons and trend analysis (which have been previously discussed).

Perhaps the simplest management perspective of analysis is that of creating summaries of data. This simple type of analysis is shown in Figure 6.13. The DSS analyst has looked at raw data in the data warehouse and has created a summary for management. Management finds summaries useful because it capsulizes data for them. Summarization presents data to management quickly and concisely.

However the conciseness of summarization is received, management typically wants to be able to "peel the onion back" and look at successively lower levels of detail. This

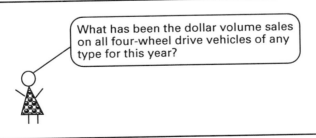

Figure 6.13.   Creating summaries.

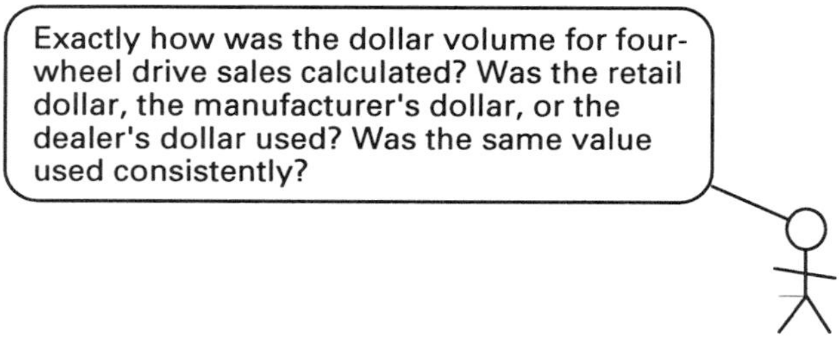

Exactly how was the dollar volume for four-wheel drive sales calculated? Was the retail dollar, the manufacturer's dollar, or the dealer's dollar used? Was the same value used consistently?

Figure 6.14. Doing drill-down analysis.

peeling back of the onion is called "drill-down analysis" and is shown in Figure 6.14.

Management starts with some summary figure of interest. Then they want to find out what data went into the summary. Or management wants to know exactly how the calculation was made in the first place. Of course, once management starts to view the data at the lower level of summary, there is the possibility that they will want to go to an even lower level of analysis.

Perhaps the most sophisticated analysis that takes place on the data found in the warehouse is the *complex correlation*. An example is shown in Figure 6.15. On the one hand, complex correlations can lead to very important and sophisticated conclusions. There is a tremendous potential payback in the creation and interpretation of a complex correlation. On the other hand, complex correlations are

- difficult to construct,
- subject to misinterpretation, and
- fragile in the best of cases.

Whatever the difficulties there are associated with complex correlations, when one is constructed that meets

When a model year has included air bags, have the sales been higher or lower than comparable model years when air bags have not been included, and by how much? And what is the difference between including single air bags and dual air bags?

Figure 6.15. Looking for complex correlations.

management needs, the results can be spectacular as management is given a new insight in how to better run the business.

There are many combinations and permutations of the basic query types that have been described here. The DSS analyst is limited only by his or her imagination.

DISPLAYING THE RESULTS

There are as many ways to display the results of a query as there are ways to create the query. Figure 6.16 shows a few of the common ways in which the results of a query are displayed. The display of the query is relative to the point being made by the analyst. In the case that the DSS analyst wants to deliver a single "answer" to management, a single report with a single piece of information may suffice. In other cases, the DSS analyst may want to make the point that there is no one answer, but a general correlation. Here, the analyst delivers the information in a form as complex as a scatter diagram. The form of display is determined by the message and the analysis the DSS analyst wishes to deliver.

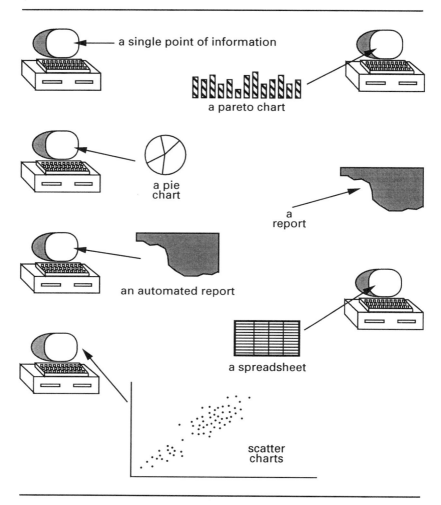

Figure 6.16. Some common ways information is delivered.

PUTTING THE ANALYSIS INTO "PRODUCTION"

Once the DSS analyst has completed the original analysis, there remains the issue of whether to do it over again. In some cases, the analysis that was created is truly a onetime activity. In other cases, the DSS analyst creates an analysis that is going to be of continuing usefulness to the corporation. When the DSS analyst has created an analysis that needs to be run repeatedly, there are several options, as shown in Figure 6.17. The repeated analysis can take several forms—a single report that is run periodically, a series of reports, a periodically run analysis where data is collected as a byproduct of execution, and so forth.

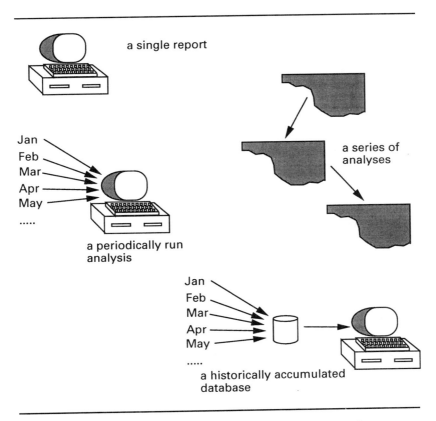

Figure 6.17.   Some methods of scheduling reports and analyses.

There are some considerations when putting an analysis into production:

- Does the entire analysis need to be redone by a professional technician? Often times the analysis created by the DSS analyst is good for a single report, but needs to be reshaped if the report is to be run repeatedly.
- Does data need to be periodically collected for the purposes of creating the report? If so, should the data be placed in a data warehouse or elsewhere?
- What are the procedures that need to be set into motion to insure the periodic recreation of the analysis?
- Who is going to be the recipient of the analysis? How does the analysis reach the recipient?
- Who is going to pay for the ongoing analysis?

SUMMARY

In the usage of the data warehouse and the ODS, the creation of the analysis by the DSS is where the payoff is. There are four important components in the world of the DSS analyst:

- the statement or understanding of the business problem,
- the metadata that exists to describe what the possible candidates of data are for the solving of the business problem,
- the query tool that serves as the interface between the DSS analyst and the data warehouse, and
- the data warehouse itself.

The requirements for the statement and understanding of the business problem are generally time boxed, since the analysis conducted by the DSS analyst will be done in a heuristic fashion. The DSS analyst "fishes in the right pond" by looking for analytical opportunities in

- finance,
- marketing,
- sales,
- actuary,
- engineering, and
- customer profiling.

7

Using Information for Competitive Advantage: Some Examples

Throughout this book it has been declared that informational processing has a real and positive effect on the bottom line of profitability of the corporation. The assertion has been made that informational processing should be one of the most important tools for survival of the corporation. This chapter will illustrate why informational processing has such appeal. Examples of the role of informational processing will be given for a variety of industries in different circumstances.

In almost every case, the data warehouse is at the heart of informational processing. In some cases, the ODS is at the heart of informational processing. Architecture—in whatever form—sets the stage for effective informational processing. It is as simple as this: When there is an architected approach to data and information processing, the corporation is able to do effective informational processing. But when there is no architecture, informational processing is not possible.

A STEEL MANUFACTURER

Steel is manufactured in units of "heats" or "batches." At the end of the smelting and refining of a heat of steel, the usable amount of steel is measured against the unusable amount. The result is a ratio called a "yield." If all the steel from a heat is usable, then the yield is 100 percent. If 20 percent of the steel is unusable, then the yield would be 80 percent. Obviously, the higher the yield, the more productive the steel company.

A given heat may have up to 40,000 variables of information attached to it. The chemical content, the "gauge" of the steel, and the temperature are all measured in the manufacturing process. Most of the 40,000 variables that are measured are captured as the steel is rolled out. Every twelve inches a measurement is taken.

Figure 7.1 shows the information dimension of the steel manufacturing process. When a steel company can produce higher yield (especially where the higher yield can be created for little or no marginal cost) then the bottom line of the steel company is affected positively. Engineers capture both yield information and the 40,000 variables of manufacturing and store the information in a data warehouse. The in-

• Steel is manufactured in "heats" or batches.

• Each batch has up to 40,000 variables.

• Each batch has a "yield."

Figure 7.1.   A steel manufacturer.

"What were the top ten yields this year?
the bottom ten yields?"

"What factors contributed to a good yield?
a bad yield?"

Figure 7.2.   The engineer's analysis.

tent is to allow the engineer to analyze the factors that con-
tribute to both high and low yields. Figure 7.2 shows an
engineer correlating what goes into a good or bad heat.

Interestingly, both good and bad factors are equally
important to the engineer. Simply by determining what factors relate to higher and lower yields, the engineer can improve the manufacturing process with no further capital
investment.

Unfortunately, because of the number of variables associated with each heat, doing a statistically significant analysis
is not easy. In the best of circumstances the engineer has a
complex task in capturing and analyzing the many variables.

One factor complicating the life of the engineer is that
managing 40,000 variables for each heat soon adds up to a
lot of data. Not only are there 40,000 variables per heat, but
there are many heats that must be considered as well. The
sheer volume of data to be analyzed by the engineer starts to
present its own barrier.

The data warehouse that is created for the engineer is
designed to accommodate the large volumes of data. Not
doing this from the outset is a mistake. Figure 7.3 shows the
structure of the data warehouse.

There are three levels of data in the engineering data
warehouse. At the highest level are stored the 150 most important variables per heat. A group of experienced engineers

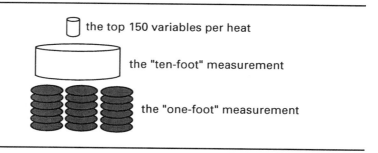

the top 150 variables per heat

the "ten-foot" measurement

the "one-foot" measurement

Figure 7.3.   The hierarchy of storage for the engineer's
manufacturing data warehouse.

decides what these are. These "most important" variables
are pulled from the 40,000 variables and placed on very-
high-performance storage.

By storing only 150 variables, the engineer is able to
store and compare information about many heats. And since
the "most important" data is on high-performance storage, it
is able to be easily manipulated. Comparisons across many
heats is a real possibility at this level of the data warehouse.

The next level of storage in the data warehouse is called
the "ten-foot" level, because measurements of steel quality
are taken every ten feet. This means that there are approxi-
mately 4,000 variables per heat in this midlevel of the data
warehouse. The data at this level is stored on medium speed
storage. Data is able to be accessed directly, but at a slower
speed than at the higher level of storage. Conversely, the
unit of cost of storage at the midlevel is less expensive than
the unit of storage at the high level.

The low level of the data warehouse is where the bulk
detail is stored. At the low level all 40,000 variables per heat
are stored. This low level is rarely accessed. In all but the
most unusual circumstances the engineer is able to satisfy

the analytical needs at the higher levels of the data warehouse. The low level of storage is called the "one-foot" level, because the measurements found at this level are taken every twelve inches. The low level of storage is on bulk storage. Bulk storage is inexpensive but is also slower than the technology found at higher levels. The engineer always starts the analysis at the high level and proceeds downward.

One of the interesting characteristics of steel manufacturing data warehousing is that data at the detail level normally cannot be summarized or aggregated. In many environments, as data ages the need for detail diminishes. Not so the steel manufacturing data warehouse. The details of manufacture for a heat that was done a year ago may well be as important or as interesting as the details done for a heat done yesterday.

Merely by improving the study and management of information, the steel engineer can improve the bottom line of the corporation. In addition, the improvements the engineer makes often have no further capital cost associated with them.

A CELLULAR TELEPHONE COMPANY

Several years ago the cellular telephone industry was in its infancy. In the early days of the cellular telephone industry gathering market share was the primary objective of the business. The more market share a cellular company could garner, the more long-term revenues there would be. Called "subscribers," market share was simply the most important business objective in the early days, more important than profitability.

Cellular companies competed for market share in the traditional ways—by advertising and by promotion. A typical ad would be "Sign up for cellular services this week and get your first thirty days usage at a 50 percent discount."

These promotions not only brought in new customers, but also conditioned the customer to use the cellular service.

One cellular telephone company took an architected approach to the management of information. The architecture shown in Figure 7.4 is the classical architecture that is centered around a data warehouse.

The cellular company found that it could produce reports from its architecture in a very effective way. Typically, within 24 hours of the close of a promotion, an analysis of the promotion would be made for the appropriate district marketing manager. The report would be produced quickly, would be customized, would reflect true corporate information, and would contain credible information. A typical report is shown in Figure 7.5.

There were three essential components to the customized decision-support reports:

a = the actual number of subscribers that signed up during the life of the promotion

b = the number of subscribers expected to have signed up had there been no promotion

c = the actual cost of the promotion

From these simple numbers an "effectiveness ratio" was calculated:

$(a-b)/c$ = the effectiveness ratio

The higher the ratio, the more effective the promotion. The lower the ratio, the less effective the promotion.

The effectiveness ratio was calculated almost immediately at the close of a promotion. The information was delivered to the responsible marketing analyst. By giving quantified, reliable, and quick feedback to the marketing

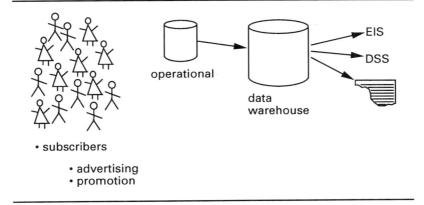

• subscribers

   • advertising
   • promotion

Figure 7.4.   The information systems architecture for a cellular telephone company.

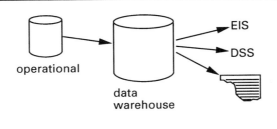

a typical report -

   a = actual number of new subscribers
   b = expected new subscribers with no promotion
   c = actual cost of promotion

   $\dfrac{a-b}{c}$ = effectiveness ratio of promotion

Figure 7.5.   How information was used to improve market share.

analyst, the analyst was able to judge how best to approach his or her district. In some places, advertising on the radio in the morning during drive time was the most cost-effective solution. In other cases, the marketing analyst found that advertising on television was the most cost-effective solution. In still other districts, the marketing analyst found that advertising in the newspaper was the most effective.

Only through having credible, timely, and customized information was the marketing analyst able to determine how best to approach a given district.

Informational processing led to the ability to attract a larger market share less expensively than if it had not been available.

A CLOTHING MANUFACTURER/RETAILER

A clothing manufacturer/retailer has built many applications over the years. Part of each application is financial information. Some applications report on one thing; other applications report on other things. Furthermore, they have been maintained to the point that they are very shopworn. Figure 7.6 illustrates the clothing manufacturer/retailer's environment, depicting the classical "spider web" of application systems. The ability of management to have a report is no problem—management can access any number of reports. Instead, management desires a report that is credible. Each of the many applications has its own limited perspective of the corporation and its own set of reports. But management is reluctant to believe any one report because there is so much conflicting information.

In addition, when management wishes to have a corporate perspective of the workings of the company, there is nowhere to turn. Trying to create a corporate report on the basis of the architecture shown in Figure 7.6 is equally frustrating. The many applications making up the legacy sys-

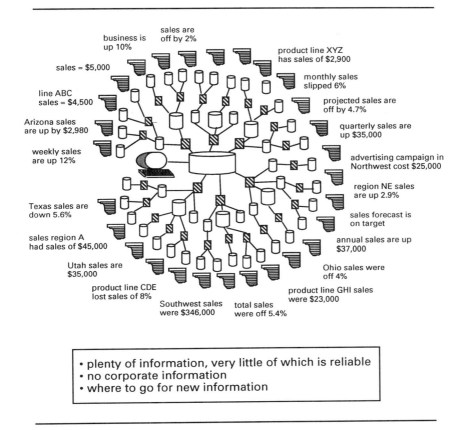

Figure 7.6.   A clothing manufacturer (part 1).

tems environment were never built to support a corporate perspective, so it is no surprise that trying to superimpose a corporate mask over them is not a successful strategy.

After a long period of trying everything to avoid confronting the older legacy systems, the clothing manufacturer/retailer adopts the stance of building a data warehouse. Figure 7.7 shows the data warehouse that is built from the older legacy systems environment.

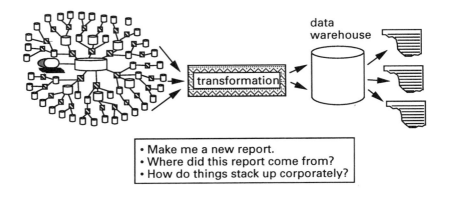

Figure 7.7. A clothing manufacturer (part 2).

Once the data warehouse is built, management can at long last start to

- build new reports easily,
- look at things from a corporate perspective, and
- understand the perspective of a given report.

By getting information into the hands of the corporation (in particular, corporate management), whole new vistas begin to open up. Management can see how one region compares with another and how the introduction of a new product line is faring. Management can anticipate financial problems before the problems become large and painful. In short, *corporate* information allows management to see things that were previously unobservable as long as they operated from reports that came from the unintegrated, corporate spider web. Now corporate management is in the position to make informed, corporate decisions.

A MULTINATIONAL COMPANY

A large multinational company has subsidiaries in many different locations around the globe. In many ways these foreign offices are autonomous. The conduct of business varies significantly from one country to the next. In that regard there is a valid reason for separating the business according to country. In some ways, the different subsidiaries form a larger company in name only.

However, corporate management has a need to measure the company as a company, and there is a need to integrate at least basic financial information across the world, even if the subsidiaries are autonomous. Figure 7.8 illustrates the multinational company.

From the standpoint of technology, there is no uniformity whatsoever from one subsidiary to another. One country operates on large mainframe computers. Another subsidiary operates on minicomputers. Another subsidiary operates on distributed processors, and so forth. The technological environment can be described as extremely heterogeneous.

In order to achieve integration, at least at the financial level, the multinational company decides to implement a data warehouse. The corporate data warehouse is to be housed in headquarters. Each of the subsidiaries produces its own "staged" data warehouse file. The staged data warehouse file lifts data from the subsidiary and transforms the data into the corporate format. In addition, the technological conversion is made in pulling data from the subsidiaries technology and reformatting it into the technology of the corporate data warehouse.

After the staged data warehouse is created at the subsidiary, it is transported to the headquarters and loaded into the corporate data warehouse. Figure 7.9 shows the movement of integrated, transformed data out of the subsidiary and into the corporate data warehouse.

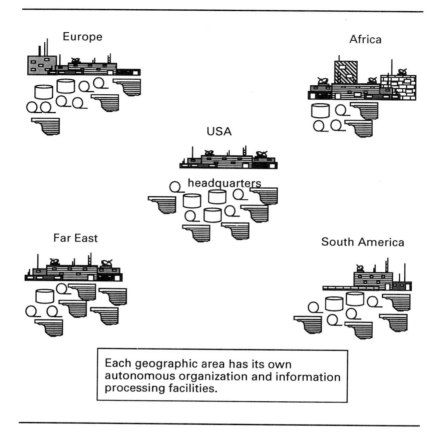

Figure 7.8. A multinational company (part 1).

Once the corporate data warehouse is loaded, consolidated reporting can now be done from the warehouse. Figure 7.10 shows the consolidated reports that ensue.

The data warehouse discussed here is unusual in that the detail data resides at the subsidiary level. In essence, the data that is sent to the corporate data warehouse is transformed and to some extent lightly summarized. Most data warehouses do not exhibit this property.

Once the corporate data warehouse is loaded, manage-

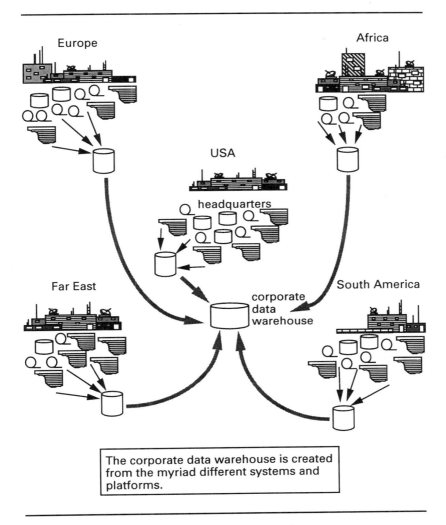

The corporate data warehouse is created from the myriad different systems and platforms.

Figure 7.9.   A multinational company (part 2).

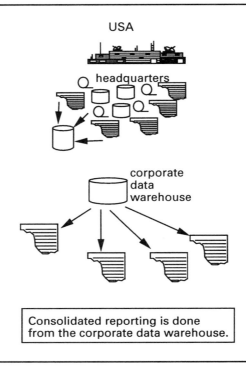

USA

headquarters

corporate
data
warehouse

Consolidated reporting is done
from the corporate data warehouse.

Figure 7.10. A multinational company (part 3).

ment finds that it can look at things in a corporate fashion
as never before. Now truly global decisions can be made,
based on facts gleaned from the corporate data warehouse.

How much is it worth to a multinational corporation to
be able to view itself globally? The value is measured in
percents of profit on the balance sheet.

A TELEMARKETING MAIL-ORDER
RETAIL COMPANY

A telemarketing mail-order company regularly sends out
catalogs in order to advertise its goods. When a consumer
receives the catalog, he or she peruses it and calls an 800

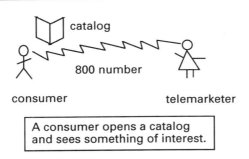

Figure 7.11.   A telemarketing retail company (part 1).

number for further information. Waiting for the call is a telemarketer. Figure 7.11 illustrates the sales process of the retail mail-order company.

The scenario depicted could fit any number of companies. However, the retail mail-order company has in the background a data warehouse. Figure 7.12 shows the data warehouse that has been built.

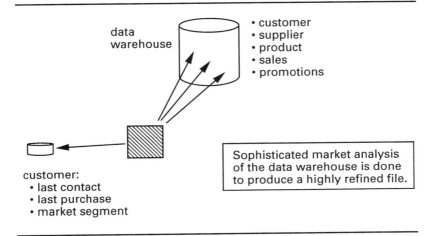

Figure 7.12.   A telemarketing retail company (part 2).

The data warehouse contains integrated historical information about many things important to the retailer, such as customer information, supplier information, product information, sales information, and promotional information. The data warehouse has been built from the record of the many activities of the company over the years.

Analyzing the data warehouse is a set of very sophisticated programs that examine the contents of the data warehouse. The marketing programs analyze the data warehouse from many perspectives. One of the files produced periodically by the marketing analysis programs is a small "distilled" customer file.

The distilled customer file essentially provides answers to three types of questions:

- When was the last time the retailer had contact with the customer?
- What was the last purchase the customer made?
- What marketing categories does the customer fit into?

The last of these pieces of information is really a sophisticated guess as to whether the customer is a

- country dweller/city dweller,
- parent of a boy/of a girl,
- hiker,
- tennis player,
- golfer,
- sailor,
- man/woman,
- professional/blue collar, and so forth.

Based on the demographic analysis done, the marketing category is loaded into the distilled customer file. When the customer calls in response to the catalog, the distilled customer file is waiting. The telemarketer greets the customer: "It's nice to hear from you again, Mr. Inmon. I see that we haven't heard from you since last April."

Then the telemarketer continues

> "How was that blue golf sweater you bought last year? Was it warm enough? Did it stretch while you were swinging?"

The consumer is amazed that the retailer really "knows" him or her. The effect of the first two pieces of information in the distilled customer file is to "personalize" what would otherwise be an anonymous conversation. This personalization goes a long way to make the consumer feel that he or she is a unique and valued customer.

After the personalization has been done, the telemarketer continues:

> "I am really glad you called today. It is quite a coincidence that we just got in some new golf balls that travel further than any others when hit. We haven't advertised them in our catalogs. In fact, we may never advertise them. I see that you are a golfer Mr. Inmon: how would you like for me to include a dozen of these special golf balls along with your order today?"

The telemarketer knows what marketing category the consumer fits into, and after personalizing the conversation, it is a simple matter to directly sell to that category.

Unquestionably, using information in the retail environment raises the revenues of the retailer. Top line revenues are enhanced by a simple use of information. Interestingly, the cost of creating an informational environment is very little in terms of capital expenditures. Other than the cost of the equipment to support the data warehouse, there are no other significant capital expenditures. Yet, the return on the investment of using information may raise corporate revenues by as much as 10 percent.

This form of informational processing is interesting in that it shows how information from the data warehouse is used in an operational environment. Data is analyzed and cultivated from the data warehouse and is distilled into a separate file that fits into the company's operational systems.

AN AIRLINE

An airline has an arrangement with the travel agents that it works with such that upon the making of a booking the commission paid the travel agent is variable. When the travel agent calls to see if a booking can be made, the airline agent confirms that a seat is available and what the commission will be.

The airline finds that if it quotes too low of a commission the travel agent takes business to other airlines. On the other hand, if the airline agent quotes too high of a commission, the airline is giving away money. It is in the airline's best interest to carefully calculate a proper and optimal commission. Figure 7.13 shows the interchange between the travel agent and the airline ticketing agent.

In order to calculate the optimal commission, two basic pieces of information are necessary—current bookings for the flight in question, and historical bookings. In other words, if there are historically plenty of seats available, the airline agent wants to quote a high commission in order to entice the travel agent to make the booking. On the other hand, if the flight is historically booked, then the airline wants to quote a low commission rate.

It is noteworthy that current flight bookings are high or low only relative to historical bookings. Without historical bookings, the airline agent really does not know whether a flight is overbooked or underbooked.

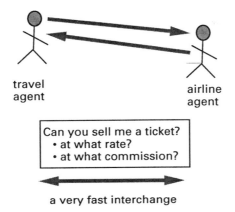

travel agent

airline agent

Can you sell me a ticket?
• at what rate?
• at what commission?

a very fast interchange

If the ticket commission is too low, the travel agent will take the business elsewhere.

If the ticket commission is too high, the airline is giving away money.

the stakes involved in calculating ticket commission correctly

Figure 7.13.   An airplane (part 1).

Two files of information are available to the airline agent—the current flight information and the data warehouse. The current flight information is kept in a high-performance system and is readily available to the airline agent. However, the historical sales of flights is stored in the data warehouse. Periodically, the data warehouse is scanned and the up-to-the-minute status of the flight is calculated. In order to do this historical analysis, it is necessary to scan *millions* of records. The result of the scan and analysis is the creation of a small flight status file. The flight status file is updated and made available in the online, high-performance

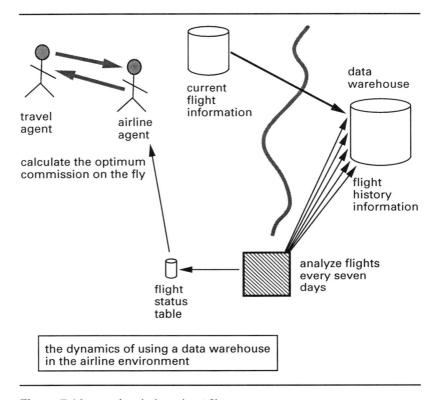

the dynamics of using a data warehouse in the airline environment

Figure 7.14. An airplane (part 2).

portion of the operational environment. Figure 7.14 shows the dynamics of the calculation of flight status.

Once the airline agent wants to calculate a commission, he or she goes to the current flight file to get current booking information, then to the flight status file to get the historical perspective of information. The two pieces of information are quickly gathered and compared and the optimal commission is calculated on the spot. The use of information allows the airline to dynamically and accurately calculate commission in its relationship with the travel agent. The bottom line of the airline is thus enhanced by the use of information.

A MIDSIZE MANUFACTURER

A midsize manufacturer decides to analyze its expenditures on data processing (DP). Much to the chagrin of the manufacturer, it is discovered that the revenues being spent on data processing are rising very quickly (and have been for some time). At one time, the amount of money spent on data processing was only a small fraction of the corporate budget. But a simple comparison shows that corporate DP expenditures are rising at a much faster rate than corporate revenues. No longer is information systems a speck on the corporate budget.

The constant rise in DP expenditures causes concern in the executive levels of the corporation. A deeper analysis of DP expenditures soon follows. It is discovered that the cost of operational processing has risen at about the rate of corporate growth for the past several years. The single largest growing expenditure in DP is the amount of money spent on 4GL processing. The amount of money spent on end-user 4GL processing is rising—year after year—at around 40 percent per annum. Needless to say, this rise is much faster than the corporate revenues. Figure 7.15 shows these spending trends.

The 4GL reporting is being done by the end user on a foundation of old, legacy systems. In many ways, this is not a good fit. The older legacy systems were designed to support operational requirements, not reporting requirements. The technology of the older legacy systems is primarily transactional. Reporting is not run in units of transactions. The data is organized in the older legacy systems to support efficient access of a single record in a random way. The 4GL reporting is done by accessing many records sequentially. There is a

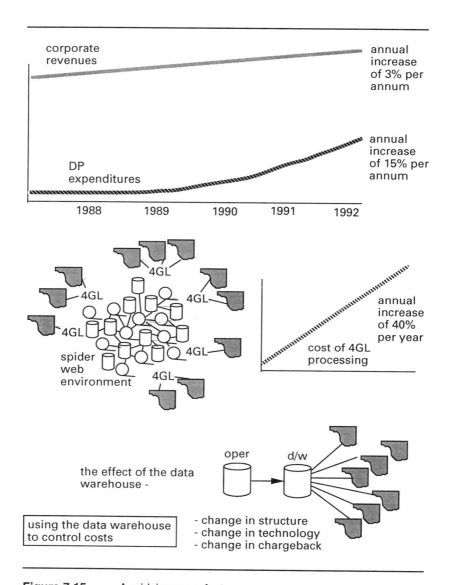

Figure 7.15. A midsize manufacturer.

very uncomfortable fit between the older legacy applications and the collar of reporting that had been placed on the legacy systems long after the legacy systems were built.

The suggestion is made to create a data warehouse as a foundation for corporate reporting to ease the financial crunch caused by 4GL reporting against the old applications. There are various reasons why the data warehouse will ease the financial burden of the manufacturer:

- The data warehouse can be optimized for reporting, something not possible in the spider web environment. The optimization of reporting processing means that reports will run much more efficiently.
- The data warehouse contains corporate, integrated data. Many fewer reports will be required and those that are built will be much simpler than if they were run in the legacy systems environment.
- The data warehouse can be put on a separate platform. The platform may well cost less to run on and execute on than the platform the legacy systems are running on.
- Removing reporting from the legacy systems environment will free up precious CPU cycles.
- Chargeback is easier to implement in a data warehouse environment than it is in a legacy systems, spider web environment.

The simple move to a data warehouse begins to reduce DP expenditures almost immediately.

AN INSURANCE COMPANY

An insurance company's executives become enamored of Executive Information Systems (EIS). The executives purchase a popular EIS package and inform the IS manager that it is the IS manager's job to install the EIS environment.

The IS manager follows the lead of management and installs the EIS. But the minute the IS manager starts to load data into the EIS from the legacy systems environment, the manager finds that it is *much* harder to deal with the data going into the EIS than it is to install and support the EIS itself. Figure 7.16 depicts the dilemma of IS management.

In a word, the insurance company finds that there is a very uncomfortable fit between the needs of EIS and the older legacy, spider web systems that contain the corporation's data.

As time passes, the fit between EIS and older legacy systems gets no better. One day, the insurance company decides that a new foundation of data is in order if it is to support EIS properly, and embarks on the building of a data warehouse. Once the data warehouse begins to be populated, the insurance company encounters a pleasant surprise—EIS fits on top of a foundation of data warehouse very comfortably, better than they had imagined. Figure 7.17 illustrates the fit between EIS and data warehouse. The data ware-

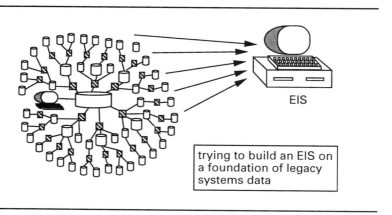

EIS

trying to build an EIS on a foundation of legacy systems data

Figure 7.16. An insurance company (part 1).

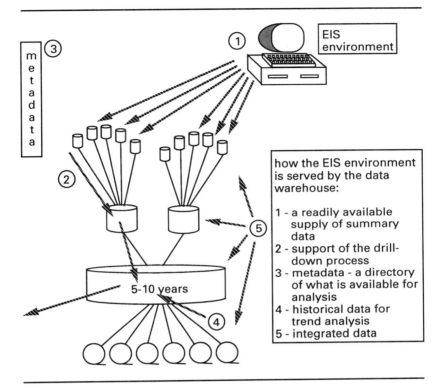

how the EIS environment is served by the data warehouse:

1 - a readily available supply of summary data
2 - support of the drill-down process
3 - metadata - a directory of what is available for analysis
4 - historical data for trend analysis
5 - integrated data

Figure 7.17.   An insurance company (part 2).

house provides a rich supply of summary data. This summary data is useful for satisfying the needs of management that is constantly changing its mind as to what is important. One day management is interested in finance, the next instant management is interested in production, then competition. The data warehouse is the best line of defense in the satisfaction of restless management.

Another reason why the EIS is supported so well by the data warehouse is the *drill-down process*. When management finds something that catches their attention, they naturally want to know more about the details. The very structure of the data warehouse—going from highly summarized data to lightly summarized data to detailed data—is precisely the architecture that is needed for drill-down processing.

EIS is also supported by the data warehouse through the existence of metadata. Metadata allows the DSS analyst using the data warehouse to be proactive in the search for data and information, as we have already seen in Chapter 6.

Another way that EIS is supported by the data warehouse is in the existence of large amounts of historical data. This is exactly what management needs in order to do trend analysis. Indeed, without a rich supply of historical data, trend analysis is merely wishful thinking.

Finally, the data in the warehouse is corporate. As data enters the data warehouse it is integrated and transformed from its application legacy foundation into a real corporate format. It is this corporate data that management wants to see and examine. When management asks for a corporate report, there is no need to thrash between applications in order to produce the report. In the older legacy systems environment, the majority of the report development effort is spent in thrashing through the different applications in order to produce the reports.

There is, then, a very good fit between EIS and data warehouse. The information provided by the data warehouse and delivered to management by means of the EIS more than pays for itself. Once the data warehouse is installed as a foundation for it, management starts to enjoy the fruits of EIS.

A CREDIT SCORING SYSTEM

A financial institution wishes to do "online" credit application processing. The concept is that a customer walks up to a teller and the teller approves (or disapproves) the request for credit on the spot. The customer knows immediately where he or she stands. The problem is that there is a fair amount of analysis that needs to go into a credit approval. Very seldom is credit analysis a straightforward decision. Nevertheless, the financial institution feels it will gain an advantage in the marketplace by being able to do online credit approval.

The financial institution creates a customer data warehouse. The customer data warehouse can be characterized as being both large and eclectic. Analyzing the data warehouse for creditworthiness is more of an art than a science. Many different pieces of different types of data must be considered collectively in order to do the analysis properly.

The financial institution creates a series of analysis programs that scan and compare the customer data warehouse periodically. Then the analysis programs produce a small file that prequalifies a customer for a loan. The prequalified loan file is then made available to the teller in the online environment. Figure 7.18 shows the credit scoring system and the customer data warehouse.

When the customer walks up to the teller and asks for credit approval, the teller merely enters the prequalified file and determines whether the loan can be approved.

"On-the-spot" loan analysis and approval allows the financial institution to expand its offerings and its market share, with little or no capital expense.

A RETAILER

A large national retailer wishes to engage in online inventory management. The retailer has stores throughout the United States, as shown in Figure 7.19. The retailer wishes to do online inventory management for at least two reasons:

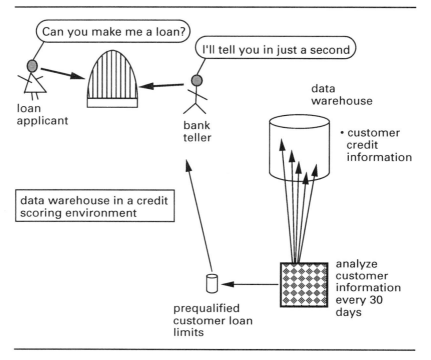

Figure 7.18. A credit scoring system.

- By doing up-to-the-second inventory management the retailer can spot trends quickly.
- By doing corporatewide inventory management the retailer can take advantage of buying in volume.

It is believed that doing a good job of online inventory management will yield a competitive advantage that will significantly and positively affect the bottom line of the corporation. The problem is that the retailer has many stores that are geographically dispersed. Each of the stores has its own way of handling inventory. The logistics of transporting the inventory figures back to corporate and then assimilating those numbers into an integrated whole is a daunting task.

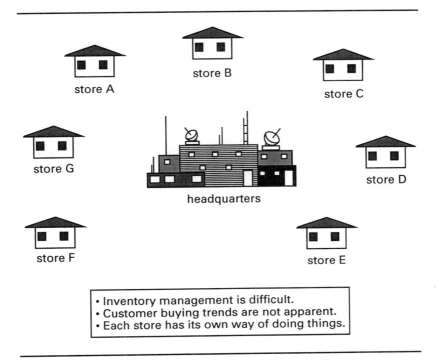

store B

store A

store C

store G

store D

headquarters

store F

store E

- Inventory management is difficult.
- Customer buying trends are not apparent.
- Each store has its own way of doing things.

Figure 7.19. Online inventory management (part 1).

Among other things, a basic transformation of data must be done as the data comes out of each store. Figure 7.20 depicts this transformation. Raw data is not transmitted to the headquarters. Instead, the raw store data is refined at the store level. This transformation includes such activities as rekeying data if necessary, editing transactions, and summarizing some types of data. Once the data has been properly conditioned, it is then forwarded to headquarters.

Once at headquarters, the data is stored in an ODS, not a data warehouse. The ODS is updated as soon as it arrives. In truth very little actual update is done. Almost all of the activity is appended to the ODS.

Once the data has been gathered into the ODS, the cor-

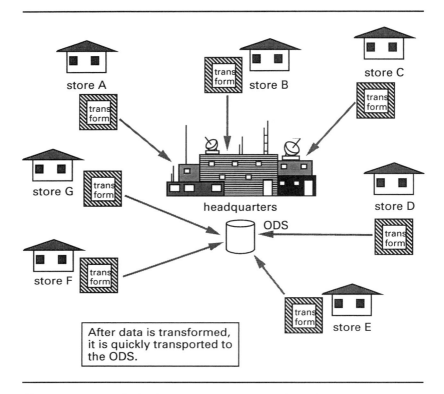

store A

trans form

store B

store C

trans form

trans form

store G

trans form

headquarters

ODS

store D

trans form

store F

trans form

trans form

store E

After data is transformed, it is quickly transported to the ODS.

Figure 7.20. Online inventory management (part 2).

porate analysts are able to consider the data on a collective, corporatewide basis. Figure 7.21 shows the kinds of reporting and analysis that can be generated from the ODS.

This example of informational processing differs from the norm in that informational reporting is done from an ODS, not a data warehouse. The fact that processing is done from an ODS, however, does nothing to diminish the value of informational processing. Indeed, the timeliness of the information is such that an ODS is the only way to achieve the goals of the company.

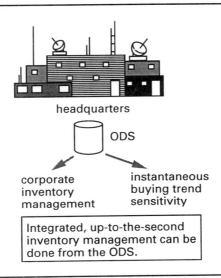

headquarters

ODS

corporate
inventory
management

instantaneous
buying trend
sensitivity

Integrated, up-to-the-second
inventory management can be
done from the ODS.

Figure 7.21.   Online inventory management (part 3).

SUMMARY

There are many ways to use informational processing in
many types of companies. In some cases, informational processing is done for the purpose of creating credible reports.
In other cases, informational processing is done to achieve
corporate integration.

Another way informational processing is used is at the
operational level. In this case, the data warehouse is used as
a basis for a small derivative file that resides in the operational environment.

Finally, operational processing is done not only from the
data warehouse but from the ODS as well.

8

Administering the Data Warehouse Environment

An essential ingredient of the success of the data warehouse environment is the human factor. The best designs and the best architectures in the world are of little use if there are not people available and prepared to put the plans into action.

The data warehouse environment is administered by an organizational unit called the data architecture group. The data architecture group sometimes is part of data administration. In other cases, the data architecture group stands alone. The data architecture group is neither a systems group nor an applications group—it lies outside those traditional turfs.

The data architecture group interfaces with top management, IS management, the IS organization, and the end user. The data architecture group is responsible ultimately for the success or failure of the data warehouse. The ongoing activities of monitoring the data warehouse, adding new subject areas to the data warehouse, making sure the end user is satisfied, and other activities are in the domain of the data architecture organization.

This chapter will discuss some of the principle duties and activities that are part and parcel of the administration of the data warehouse/ODS environment.

ASSISTING THE END USER

The first and most important responsibility of the data architecture group is that of making sure the end user has the best chance at using the data warehouse successfully. Anything that is a barrier to the end user's success is a problem for the data architect. The kinds of activities that are included in this category are shown in Figure 8.1.

The data architect needs to help the end user find out where data is. And when new data is populated into the data

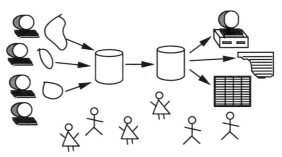

helping the user to:
• find new data
• create and execute a query
• log onto the system
• understand what has been done
• find a "lost" query
• interpret data
• plan a complex analysis
• train new users

Figure 8.1.   Administration to help the end user.

warehouse, it is up to the data architect to alert the end user to the new possibilities. If the end user has difficulty in executing a query or an analysis, the data architect should be available for help. Whether the difficulty with the query is a technical barrier or a misunderstanding as to where data is, it is up to the data architect to get the end user back on the path of productive use of the data warehouse. Even helping the end user do such simple things as logging onto the system is within the domain of the data architect.

Should an end user execute a query and not understand what has happened—either too much data has come back or no data at all has been returned—the data architect is ready to interpret what has transpired. On occasion, the end user will submit a query that never returns. The data architect is prepared to assist the end user in tracking down the "lost" query.

On occasion an end user will complete a query and not understand the results. The data architect will assist the end user in deciphering what has gone on inside the computer. Should the end user need to plan a complex analysis, the data architect is available to suggest plans of attack. As new end users come into the data warehouse environment, the data architect is on hand to get them started.

MONITORING THE DATA WAREHOUSE

The data warehouse needs to be monitored occasionally, as outlined in Figure 8.2. There are several reasons why monitoring is essential:

- The growth of data in the warehouse may be extending the limits of the technology the data warehouse is built on.
- The end user needs to know the best way to access data.
- The original design of the system may not have accounted for the manner in which the data warehouse has actually grown.

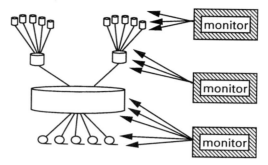

- What growth is there?
- What new summaries have been created?
- How many rows are in a table?
- What profiles of data are there?
- What data is in overflow?
- What indexes are there?
- Does a table need to be reorganized?
- Is the metadata current?
- Does edit/cleansing need to be done?
- Are error conditions detected?

Figure 8.2.   Some of the typical activities of monitoring.

- Parts of the data warehouse may contain stale data that is better kept elsewhere.

While all of the data warehouse may be monitored, it is really the current level of detail that receives the most attention. The current level of detail is where the greatest volume of data is and where the biggest investment has been made.

It is normal practice to monitor the data in the data warehouse. It is also useful to monitor the activity that is occurring in the data warehouse. Unfortunately, monitoring that activity is a technologically difficult task.

One of the reasons for monitoring the data warehouse is

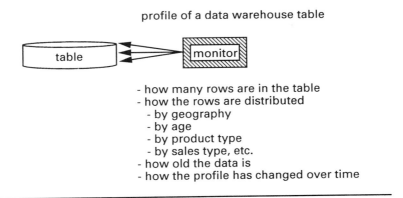

profile of a data warehouse table

- how many rows are in the table
- how the rows are distributed
  - by geography
  - by age
  - by product type
  - by sales type, etc.
- how old the data is
- how the profile has changed over time

Figure 8.3.   The profile that can be created from a monitor.

to create "profile" information, as shown in Figure 8.3. The profile of data inside the warehouse feeds the metrics that reside in the metadata. The profile information may be as simple as counting the number of rows in a table or as complex as counting different types of rows. Once the profile of data is created, the profile is made available to the end user. The end user can use the profile for many things, such as determining whether a query will be a resource hog before it is submitted, or whether the table being analyzed has any of the data being sought. The profile of the data in a data warehouse allows the end user to be proactive in the planning and design of an analysis.

In addition, the profile may keep information on the data and how it has changed over time. Keeping the time profile of data helps explain to a user why a query that ran last year in ten minutes runs this year in forty-five minutes.

An example of a time profile of data warehouse data is shown in Figure 8.4, which graphically displays the contents of the warehouse according to the different types of

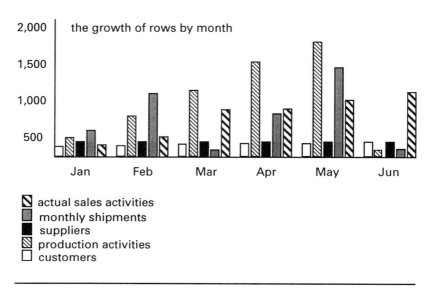

Figure 8.4.   A profile of the growth of tables by row by various categories.

data within it. Some types of data exhibit steady growth. Other tables exhibit random growth. Other tables show no growth. Still other rapidly growing tables show growth up to the point where their contents are archived and the number of rows returns to a manageable size.

Creating a time profile of data greatly helps the data architect plan how to manage the growth that occurs within the data warehouse.

DATA WAREHOUSE UTILITIES

Every data warehouse has a certain amount of standard utilities that need to be performed, such as:

- purging data,
- archiving data, and
- condensing data.

Figure 8.5 depicts the standard utilities. These fall within the domain of the data architect charged with administering the data warehouse.

In some cases, whole tables of data are purged. But where there is need to look at data a record at a time in order to determine if it should be purged, the PURGE utility is invoked. The PURGE utility uses some predetermined criteria to tell whether a record should or should not be removed from the data warehouse.

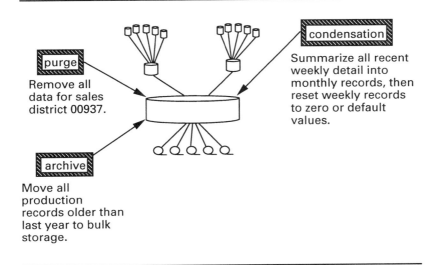

purge

Remove all data for sales district 00937.

condensation

Summarize all recent weekly detail into monthly records, then reset weekly records to zero or default values.

archive

Move all production records older than last year to bulk storage.

Figure 8.5.   Purging, archiving, and condensing data in the data warehouse.

However the purge is done—by table or a record at a time—it has been decided that the data to be purged is no longer needed for DSS analysis.

The data architect needs to make sure that space is reclaimed by the DBMS after the purge. It does little good to remove data from a data warehouse where the space formerly occupied by the data cannot be reused.

The ARCHIVE utility operates the same as the PURGE utility except that the ARCHIVE utility places the data that has been purged on another media, usually bulk storage.

The CONDENSATION utility typically combines and summarizes records and purges the detailed records. A typical condensation occurs when daily data is read and summarized into a weekly record. Then the daily data is deleted from the data warehouse.

It is through these standard utilities that the data warehouse is prevented from growing continually. These standard utilities are the data architect's first line of defense.

MAINTAINING THE METADATA

Metadata is an important component of the data warehouse. Metadata allows the end user to be proactive in the use of the warehouse. But metadata requires care and tending like all other working parts of the environment, as shown in Figure 8.6.

If a shop has a tool for the automatic upkeep of metadata such as Prism Solutions Warehouse Manager, then metadata maintenance is easy. But without some automated way to keep the metadata up to date, very soon it lags behind the progress being made in the data warehouse.

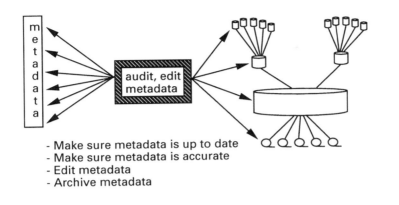

- Make sure metadata is up to date
- Make sure metadata is accurate
- Edit metadata
- Archive metadata

Figure 8.6.   Managing data warehouse metadata.

PUTTING A QUERY INTO "PRODUCTION"

Most queries start their life in the data warehouse environment in an iterative process. After some number of iterations—some formal, some informal—the query achieves a state of stability, as seen in Figure 8.7.

Once the query stabilizes, the end user may well want to run the query on a regular basis. The data architect assists

iterative
analysis

stability

Figure 8.7.   Putting the query in production.

the end user in building the procedures and setting those procedures into regular execution.

COORDINATING DEVELOPMENT
AND THE DATA MODEL

The data warehouse is under a constant state of development. If a new subject area is not being added, then a currently populated subject area is being revised. The very nature of the data warehouse is eternal development and redevelopment.

The data architect is charged with seeing that new development is integrated and harmonious with existing development. The principle tool the data architect uses for ensuring warehouse development is integrated is the *data model*. Figure 8.8 shows that the data model acts as a guideline as to how new parts of the data warehouse should be constructed.

The data architect understands how the existing data

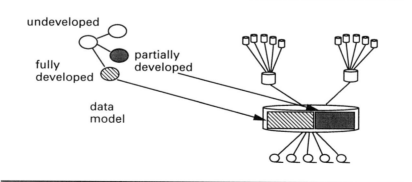

Figure 8.8.   Coordination of new development with the data model.

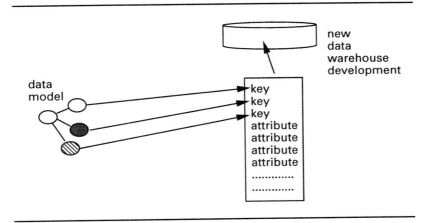

Figure 8.9.   Assuring new development is built to spec.

warehouse fits with the data model. Fitting new components of the data warehouse usually is a matter of making sure the key structure conforms to the data model and that there is no overlap of detailed data at the attribute level. Figure 8.9 shows the principle concerns of the data architect in the examination of new designs for the data warehouse.

CAPACITY PLANNING

Growth in the data warehouse is gauged at the detail level on a table-by-table basis. But growth is also gauged on a macro basis. The data architect is concerned with both the amount of storage used by the data warehouse and the amount of processing power that is consumed. Figure 8.10 shows the growth charts the data architect has produced that track the storage and processor utilization over time.

Capacity planning for the data warehouse environment

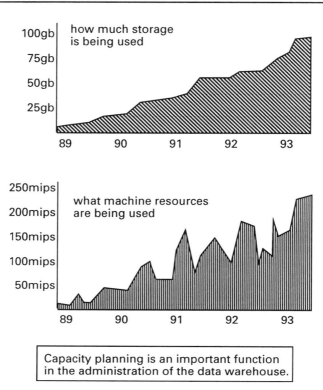

100gb | how much storage is being used
75gb
50gb
25gb
 89   90   91   92   93

250mips | what machine resources are being used
200mips
150mips
100mips
50mips
 89   90   91   92   93

Capacity planning is an important function in the administration of the data warehouse.

Figure 8.10.   Capacity planning.

is complicated by the fact that the workload for the data warehouse is essentially an accumulation of random events. In other words, detecting a constant or predictable pattern of utilization for the data warehouse workload is not a realistic expectation. (For an in-depth discussion of capacity planning in the data warehouse environment, refer to the Tech Topic on that subject by Prism Solutions.)

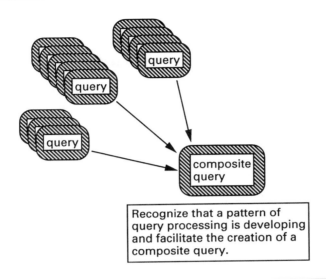

Recognize that a pattern of query processing is developing and facilitate the creation of a composite query.

Figure 8.11.   Composite queries.

CREATING COMPOSITE QUERIES

One of the best approaches to the management of the query workload is the creation of a *composite query*, as discussed in earlier chapters, and illustrated in Figure 8.11. The data architect is in the ideal position to identify the queries that should form the composite query.

The data architect looks for queries that

- are run on a regular basis,
- access the same table,
- access a large amount of data, and
- do not require immediate access.

Upon finding queries that meet these criteria, the data architect groups them together and creates the composite query.

MANAGEMENT COMMUNICATION

A very important part of the job of the data architect is that of regular management communication. Top management has a lot at stake in the building and running of the data warehouse. There needs to be constant communication between top management and the data architect, as depicted in Figure 8.12.

Top management needs to hear about both failures and successes, and needs to see where attention should be given. The data architect must be able to communicate the need for resources directly to top management. When an organization does not allow this communication to occur, the chances for success in the data warehouse environment are limited.

Communication should be directly between the data architect and top management. Having the communication travel through several lines of management is not effective.

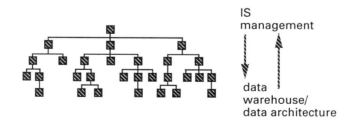

Figure 8.12.   Keeping management aware.

EIS—DATA WAREHOUSE INTERFACE

The world of EIS is strongly supported by data warehouse. But there needs to be a regular and formal relationship between the principles from each of the two worlds. The data architect needs to know when

- EIS is not working properly because of a data problem,
- EIS is not able to support an analysis because of a lack of data,
- EIS is looking elsewhere for a source of data, and so forth.

EIS needs to know when

- new data has been added to the data warehouse,
- new summarizations have been made,
- there is a change in metadata,
- there is a significant change in the volume of data for any given table, and so forth.

In short, there is a need for regular communication between the data architect and the EIS personnel. Figure 8.13 demonstrates this interchange.

SUMMARY DATA ANALYSIS AND REVIEW

Summary data in the data warehouse has the habit of growing quickly, quietly, and with no order or discipline. The data architect suddenly wakes up and there is a tremendous amount of summary data that has sprung up in the data warehouse (like weeds in the springtime).

Keeping some summary data is a good idea. But keeping all summary data that has ever been created is usually a

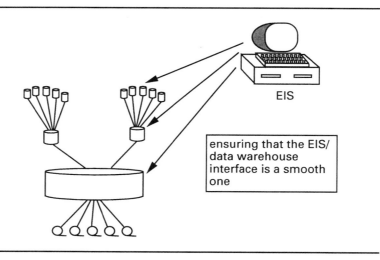

EIS

ensuring that the EIS/
data warehouse
interface is a smooth
one

Figure 8.13.   A smooth interface.

poor idea. Part of the job of the data architect is the ongoing
monitoring of the summary data portion of the data warehouse environment, outlined in Figure 8.14.

The data architect looks for

- summary data that has been created but is seldom or
  ever used thereafter,
- summary data that is the same as other summary data
  already found in the data warehouse,
- summary data that needs to be combined,
- summary data that needs to be condensed, and so forth.

ENSURING THAT NO OPERATIONAL
PROCESSING IS BEING DONE

One of the temptations that every end user faces is that of
recreating all or part of the operational environment under

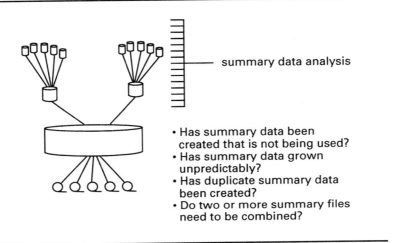

summary data analysis

- Has summary data been created that is not being used?
- Has summary data grown unpredictably?
- Has duplicate summary data been created?
- Do two or more summary files need to be combined?

Figure 8.14.   Monitoring summary data.

the guise of informational processing. The end user is given a lot of autonomy in the building and running of informational systems. What is more natural than to seize the opportunity to use the data warehouse platform and its technology to build operational systems as well as informational systems? Figure 8.15 shows the data architect constantly on the lookout for this practice.

Simply stated, the data warehouse environment is not the place for the construction and execution of operational systems. When the data architect finds the end user building operational systems in the data warehouse, he or she tactfully directs the end user to the operational environment and the application developers that work there.

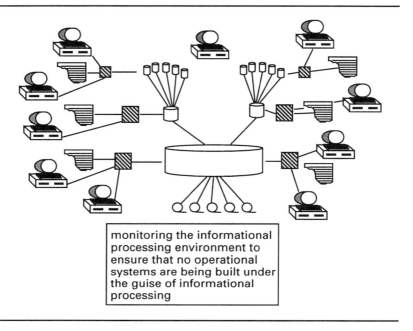

monitoring the informational
processing environment to
ensure that no operational
systems are being built under
the guise of informational
processing

Figure 8.15. Monitoring the development process.

FACTORING IN INFORMATIONAL REQUIREMENTS

From time to time the data architect is the recipient of informational requirements that have been culled from the applications development process. Figure 8.16 illustrates informational requirements being passed to the data architect from the operational environment.

These informational requirements are somewhat different from the requirements that are developed iteratively. These are the reporting requirements that have been uncovered as a result of classical applications design and require-

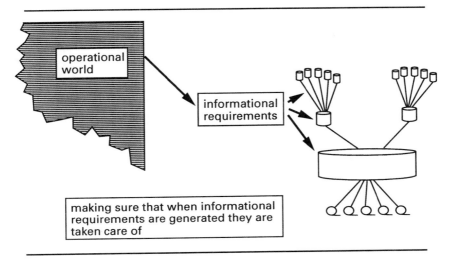

operational world

informational requirements

making sure that when informational requirements are generated they are taken care of

Figure 8.16.   Meeting information requirements.

ments analysis that come from the DSS work already being done in the production environment. It is incumbent on the data architect to consider these informational requirements in the operation of the data warehouse.

Informational requirements are usually built as a reporting application that runs on data contained in the data warehouse.

MANAGING THE TRANSFORMATION PROCESS

An essential part of the data warehouse environment is the transformation that occurs as data is passed from the operational environment to the data warehouse environment, shown in Figure 8.17.

The transformation process needs constant attention because

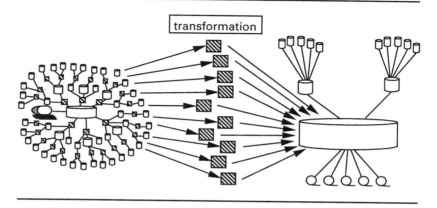

Figure 8.17. Managing the transformation process.

- it is constantly being maintained,
- the machine requirements just to run the transformation component are very large,
- the transformation process is always complex,
- the transformation process is very important to the success of the data warehouse, and so forth.

When the transformation process is automated, the data architect has a much easier task maintaining and managing the process than when the transformation process is created and maintained by hand.

MASSIVE OFF-LOADS

It is normal for a department to occasionally do a massive off-load of data from the data warehouse in order to do special DSS analysis. There are many good reasons why pulling large amounts of data away from the data warehouse can be a good design technique. The sheer reduction in volume of

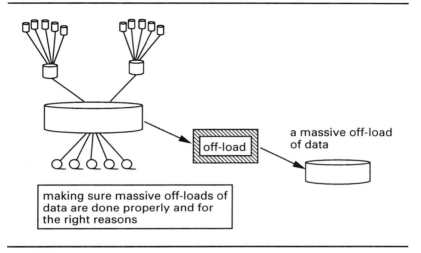

making sure massive off-loads of data are done properly and for the right reasons

Figure 8.18.   Off-loading data.

data makes all query processing more efficient, for example. Figure 8.18 shows a massive amount of data being pulled away from the data warehouse.

Just because large amounts of data are pulled from the data warehouse doesn't mean there is cause for alarm. But when the data is being pulled off on a permanent basis to reconstruct the data warehouse elsewhere, the data architect must question the motivation and the economics.

One tipoff that there is a problem is when a massive off-load of data is done on a recurring basis. If the massive off-load is done only one time, then there probably is no problem.

CORRECTING ERRORS IN THE DATA WAREHOUSE

Every now and then a data warehouse will have incorrect data entered into it. The data architect makes the correc-

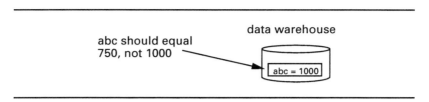

Figure 8.19.   Correcting errors when they occur.

tions. Figure 8.19 shows incorrect data in the data ware-house.

The first thing the data architect does is to determine how much bad data has entered the data warehouse. The data architect must discover the cause of the errors. Once the cause of the errors is detected and the extent of the damage is esti-mated, the data architect can then effect a solution.

SUMMARY

The data architect is responsible for the ongoing mainte-nance of the data warehouse environment. There is a lengthy and diverse list of responsibilities in this regard. Some of it is outlined here:

- Ensure end user satisfaction with the data warehouse.
- Monitor the data warehouse.
- Execute utilities such as PURGE, ARCHIVE, and CON-DENSATION.
- Keep metadata up to date.
- Put stabilized queries into production.
- Make sure new development is in line with the data model.
- Do capacity analysis and planning.
- Create composite queries where justified.
- Communicate regularly and directly with top management.

- Make sure the EIS interface is functioning properly.
- Analyze and review summary data in the warehouse.
- Monitor processing to make sure operational processing is not being done in the data warehouse.
- Receive informational requirements and make sure they are disposed of properly.
- Manage the operational/data warehouse transformation.
- Review massive off-loads.
- Do error correction in the data warehouse when necessary.

9

Migration to the Architected Environment

The discussions of architecture have focused on the role and the structure of the ODS and the data warehouse. But little has been said about how to proceed to move the legacy systems of a shop toward the realization these architectural entities. The size of this task of *migration* and the complexities involved are cause for concern. It is no small job to move the production legacy environment anywhere, with any degree of efficiency and elegance.

IN THE BEGINNING . . .

At first there was the notion that the way to achieve order and discipline was to move the production legacy systems environment into a world of *subject databases*. Figure 9.1 depicts this early vision. The notion was that subject databases would provide the integration, organization, and control that was absent from the legacy production environment. The newly minted subject databases would be integrated and the

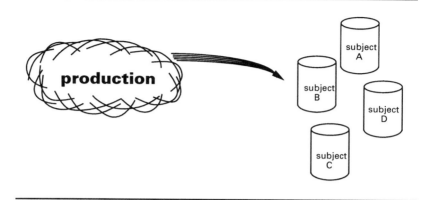

Figure 9.1.   Getting to Nirvana.

organization would benefit from the corporate perspective that naturally would follow.

The reality was that many organizations attempted to go *directly* from the older legacy production environment to subject databases, as shown in Figure 9.1. For all of the good intentions and grand designs, the track record was nothing short of dismal. For a variety of reasons, this movement was fraught with problems.

Yet, there still was a need for integrated information, regardless of what the architecture of systems and data looked like. The next natural step that shops began to take in the progression to an integrated environment was toward the data warehouse, as shown in Figure 9.2.

The data warehouse allowed the corporation to integrate data and to achieve a firm foundation for the purpose of informational processing. Furthermore, there was a rational and cost-effective path to the data warehouse. Going to the data warehouse was an evolutionary process, not a revolutionary

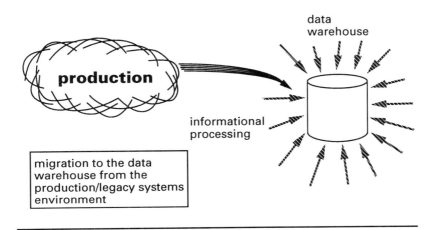

Figure 9.2.   Migrating to the data warehouse.

process. Company after company found that they could build the data warehouse in conjunction with their legacy systems. Informational processing soon began to congregate around the data warehouse. The effect was the shrinkage of the production environment, illustrated in Figure 9.3.

In the production, legacy systems environment, both the volume of data and the workload shrank. The production environment was purged of masses of old, stale archival data. The informational processing that once took place in the production, legacy systems environment migrated to the data warehouse environment. The net result was that the production systems environment was much smaller and greatly simplified.

The next step in the progression was the building of the ODS environment. Figure 9.4 depicts the ODS being built from the small, simplified production systems environment.

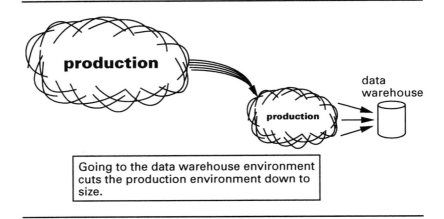

Going to the data warehouse environment cuts the production environment down to size.

Figure 9.3.   Reducing the production environment.

Because the production environment was much smaller and much more streamlined than it had been before, the building of the ODS was a relatively easy thing to do.

Naturally, the building of the ODS further shrank the production environment until the production environment

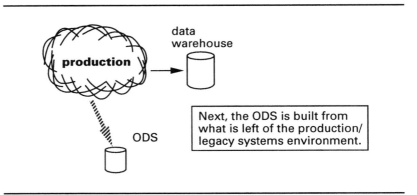

Next, the ODS is built from what is left of the production/ legacy systems environment.

Figure 9.4.   Building the ODS.

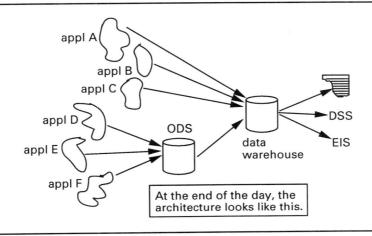

appl A

appl B

appl C

appl D

appl E   ODS

appl F

DSS

EIS

data
warehouse

At the end of the day, the
architecture looks like this.

Figure 9.5.   The resulting architecture.

was reduced to a few applications. The ODS fed the data
warehouse data when it was no longer needed for up-to-the-
second processing. The resulting architecture is shown in
Figure 9.5. Informational processing is separated from operational processing. The data warehouse is fed by both the
ODS and older application systems. Some application systems feed the ODS and other application systems never feed
the ODS, but go directly into the data warehouse. EIS, DSS,
and reporting are done from the data warehouse. Up-to-the-
second operational decisions are done from either the ODS
or from applications. The architecture shown in Figure 9.5
is one of equilibrium.

CAN THE ODS BE BUILT FIRST?

An interesting question is whether the ODS can be built
before the data warehouse is built. Figure 9.6 illustrates
that indeed the ODS can be built first. The industry track

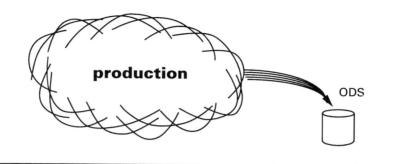

Figure 9.6.   The question of building the ODS first.

record undeniably reinforces this. But while there are some immediate operational advantages to building the ODS first, there are also some fearful obstacles:

- There is no real distinction made between operational and informational processing. It is very easy to try to use the ODS for informational processing as well as operational processing. This is always a major mistake.
- The production environment is large and bloated. The sheer volumes of data and processing that await the data architect building the ODS are awesome. Merely coping with the volumes of data presents a huge obstacle to success.
- There is the danger that the complexity of building the ODS will be so large that the corporation never gets around to building the data warehouse.

For these reasons (and undoubtedly many more) it is strongly advised that the data warehouse be built before the ODS is built.

WHAT ABOUT SUBJECT DATABASES?

What about the final target architecture that many managers set out to try to attain? What about the ideal envisioned in Figure 9.1? The architecture shown in Figure 9.5 at first glance does not look much like the subject areas that were originally intended.

And yet the architecture shown in Figure 9.5 actually *is* the subject database architecture, drawn a little differently. Figure 9.7 shows that both the data warehouse and the ODS are integrated and subject oriented. Both contain the same subjects and share the same common heritage of data modeling, and there is a regular passage of data from subject areas in the operational environment to subject areas in the data warehouse. Collectively, the subject area resides in part in the ODS and in part in the data warehouse.

Note that there is very little or no redundancy of data between the common subject areas. The ODS contains detailed, accurate, up-to-the-second data. The data warehouse contains historical data, both summary and detailed. The data found in the data warehouse once populated the ODS. But once there was no longer an operational need for the data, the data passed to the data warehouse. Indeed, the subject area goal of yesteryear is met in a very sophisticated way by the architecture displayed in Figure 9.5.

A FINAL QUESTION

Can the architecture shown in Figure 9.5 can be improved on? Is it possible to subsume the applications lying outside the ODS into the ODS? This question is illustrated in Figure 9.8.

If the applications lying outside the ODS could be subsumed by the ODS, it would be possible at long last to be rid of the legacy systems and to finally put the old production environment to rest. There is a great temptation to do what

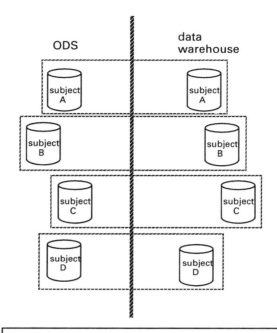

The net result of the ODS and the data warehouse is an architecture that logically fulfills the original vision.

Figure 9.7.   Nirvana revisited.

is suggested in Figure 9.8. However, there may be good reasons why applications should not be subsumed into an ODS. For example, there may be no need for corporate integration at the operational level. In this case, an ODS makes no sense.

SUMMARY

Nearly all organizations have a problem with older, legacy applications. A rational migration path is to build the data

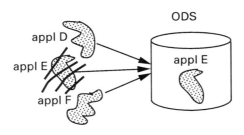

Figure 9.8.   The question of placing an application inside the ODS.

warehouse first. Building the data warehouse has the effect of shrinking the production environment in terms of workload and volumes of data.

Once the data warehouse is built, the ODS is built, further reducing the production environment. The resulting architecture is one of stability and equilibrium.

10

Connecting to the Data Warehouse

This book has covered many of the aspects of using the data warehouse, but one more remains—connecting to the data warehouse from the desktop workstation. Once the data warehouse is created, its value is often determined by the facility for accessing that warehouse from their workstations.

This chapter introduces the basic notion of desktop connectivity to remote servers (especially, data warehouses) and offers an architecture for database connectivity within the enterprise. So far, we have focused on the relationship of legacy systems to the data warehouse. This chapter explores the problems and approaches for connecting the DSS analyst to the data warehouse, as illustrated in Figure 10.1.

BASICS OF CLIENT/SERVER ARCHITECTURE

In early database systems, the application was designed and implemented to perform a custom business function for the enterprise. This application was written to an *application*

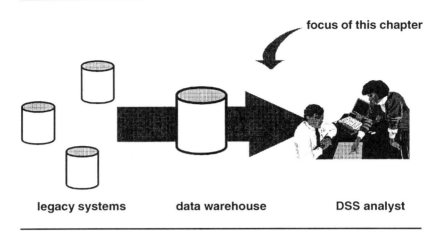

focus of this chapter

legacy systems   data warehouse   DSS analyst

Figure 10.1.   Connecting the DSS analyst to the data warehouse.

programming interface (API) specific to a certain *database management system* (DBMS). As generic applications (e.g., query tools) became available, these applications were also written using the vendor-supplied proprietary interface. Figure 10.2 illustrates this interface.

Both the application and database operated on the same platform in the early systems. Interactions between the client and server functions were tightly coupled.

With emergence of *client/server architecture* (CSA), the client application for the DSS analyst and database server for the data warehouse are on separate platforms.[1] The in-

---

[1]CSA usually implies separate platforms for client and server in real-world systems; however, a client application and database server could reside on the same platform, especially for testing and prototyping.

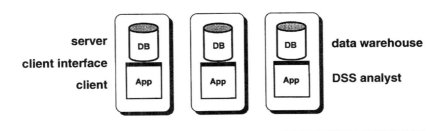

Figure 10.2.   Conventional database architecture.

teraction that occurs between the client application and the database server is shown in Figure 10.3.

The client/server architecture provides a framework for structured interaction between a client and a server. There are specific functions that the client performs (e.g., runs the application for the DSS analyst) and that the server performs (i.e., manages the data warehouse). Some of the benefits of this architecture include the support for a degree of parallel processing and the clear functional differentiation between platforms.

The interactions from the client to the server are called *requests*; the interactions from the server to the client are called *results*. In the case of relational database servers, the requests sent to the server consist of the text of SQL statements or references to previously bound SQL statements. SQL (Structured Query Language) has become the dominant query language for accessing relational databases and is supported in some standardized form by every database vendor. The results returned to the client are in the form of a flattened relational table, along with relevant status, error codes, and messages.

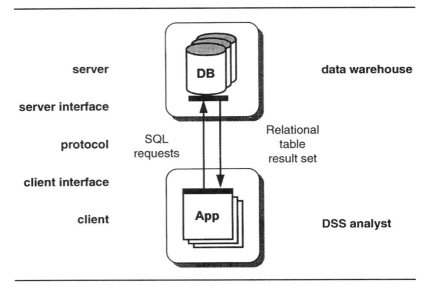

Figure 10.3.   Client/server database.

To support the request-result interaction, the client/server architecture consists of the following components:

- client interface (i.e., to the analyst's application)
- protocol
- server interface (i.e., to the data warehouse server)

First, the *client interface* is the application programming interface that the application code sees. It consists of the calling conventions, procedure/function definitions, and the syntax/semantics of the language (usually SQL) passed through the interface. The client interface accepts requests from the application logic and generates the proper protocol to convey that request to the server. In Figure 10.3, the client interface is shown as a bar on top of the client application, symbolizing the thin boundary between the application and the rest of the system. At the lowest level, a client interface is a library of procedures invoked by the client application to generate the proper protocol to the server.

All vendors offering DBMS products supply a specific client interface with their product. In most cases, the ANSI89 SQL specification defines many aspects of this client interface with other aspects designated as implementation dependent by the vendor. For example, IBM offers an SAA Common Programming Interface for SQL that evolves toward a common subset across their DBMS offerings. For COBOL programs under CICS accessing DB2 databases, IBM has a more precise specification for its client interface.

Second, the *protocol* is the stream of bits flowing on some communication transport between the two interfaces. The term *formats and protocol* (FAP) is sometimes used. Protocol consists of the sequence of commands and arguments (i.e., data structures) exchanged between the client and server, as shown in Figure 10.3 as the arrows between the client and server. Note that there is a bidirectional flow.

For example, a simple protocol would consist of a command from the client to execute immediately the SQL statement text contained in the command. The server would respond with the results of processing the SQL statement, including such information as a status code, number of columns, name and type of each column, data for first row, data for second row, and so on.

Third, the *server interface* (i.e., the interface at the data warehouse) is an interface with a role complementary to that of the client interface. Instead of responding to procedure calls from the client application, the server interface responds to the receipt of protocol "chucks" (i.e., blocks or messages). The purpose of the server interface is to accept requests from the client via the transport and pass them onto the database engine. The client interface and server interface are typically mirror images of one another; however, newer technology has allowed these interfaces to become asymmetrical, thus allowing for more interoperability among client and server platforms.

In most DBMS products, the server interface is hidden inside the database engine, implying that only that vendor's database engine can process requests using the vendor's protocol or the vendor's client interface. In the mid-1980s Sybase Corporation pioneered the concept of the Open Server, in which the server interface was offered as a separate product from the Sybase SQL Server engine. Customers could purchase the Sybase Open Server and develop client/server systems based on the Sybase architecture but not use the Sybase SQL Server engine to manage the data. Examples could be data processed from real-time sources (e.g., stock exchange quotas) or from customized ISAM files.

PORTABILITY AND INTEROPERABILITY

Two important aspects of the interaction between the DSS analyst and the data warehouse are portability and interoperability. Portability is important because from time to time it may be necessary to move the data warehouse from one platform to another, or the DSS analyst platform may change. Portability allows a change of either platform to be easily made. Likewise, interoperability is important because a data warehouse server may have to support DSS analysts on a new platform, or a DSS analyst may have to access a data warehouse on a new platform. Interoperability allows either to switch interaction with a new platform easily and reliability.

The key to achieving portability and interoperability are dependent, respectively, on interfaces and protocols. In other words, compatibility of the interfaces (client or server) determines the effort to port an application from one platform to another. The compatibility of protocols determines the effort for one system to interact with another. Hence, the interface and protocol are interdependent but should be considered distinct from one another. Any system that understands the protocol can listen to or generate requests or results, regardless of whatever interfaces may be used.

We have so far described client/server architecture as having three critical components: client interface, protocol, and server interface. This architecture can be evaluated in terms of its degree of portability and interoperability. In the next section, we discuss the problems for database connectivity when this architecture is used with proprietary interfaces and protocols.

PROBLEMS WITH PROPRIETARY ARCHITECTURES

If a corporation is concerned with only one type of client/ server architecture (i.e., all from a single vendor), then many of the problems of database connectivity disappear because we are dealing with homogeneous databases (i.e., the same database engine operating on the same platform).

A more realistic scenario for the data warehouse environment can be characterized as being *heterogeneous* and deal with *federated databases*. The data warehouse serves many different communities as well as many different levels of workers. The architecture for this environment must serve a broad and diverse community of DSS analysts.

In this case, the corporation must adopt a more *open systems* approach that accommodates the heterogeneous nature of federated databases. In the context of a client/server architecture, this open systems approach implies that the combination of client interface, protocol, and server interface must be based on published standards and supported with reliable products from a variety of vendors.

To explore the problems with a proprietary architecture, consider a situation in which an enterprise has purchased two types of servers for their data warehouses and developed DSS applications independently for each of those servers. Figure 10.4 shows the two types of servers as X and Y and two sets of applications as A and B. The first application, A, can access data in any of the databases supported by the type-X server; likewise, the second application, B, can access databases supported by the type-Y server.

This proprietary solution can be very effective within limits. But what happens when data needs to be shared among different types of database servers? In other words, how does

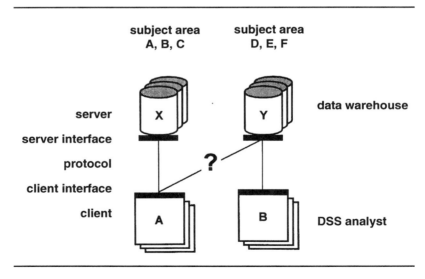

Figure 10.4.   SQL transparency.

application A access data in server type Y? In today's competitive business environment, the MIS manager that states that application A will never have to access server Y will soon have to recant those words.

In concrete terms, what changes must be made to a client application to retarget from one server to another server? We will refer to this practice as *retargeting* an application to another server. For example, if an application has been programmed to an Oracle database, what must be done to allow this application to work with IBM DB2/2? The problems with retargeting are the following:

- database interface and connection
- SQL syntax and semantics
- system catalog tables
- data types and encodings
- status codes and messages
- collating sequences
- data semantics
- transaction boundaries mismatch
- isolation levels mismatch
- user identification and privileges

To solve this new requirement, the application developer would have to program to the client interface of both server type X and server type Y. The developer would also have to change the application logic so that it is conditional on the server. For example, the SQL statement may be slightly different for each server. The test in the application program for the end of result set may be different depending on the status code returned. And if the collating sequence is different (e.g., ASCII versus EBCDIC), the sort/merge logic of the application program will generate confusing results for the user.

APPROACHES TO OPEN DATABASE CONNECTIVITY

What is the solution to this problem of proprietary architectures? There are three basic approaches (or building blocks) that potentially alleviate these serious problems:

- common interface
- common gateway
- common protocol

The secret to all three approaches is that each approach emphasizes one element *that is common* between the DSS analyst client and data warehouse server. For instance, the common-interface approach focuses on an interface (either client or server) that is common among the various server types. The common-gateway approach introduces a database gateway as the common element. Finally, the common-protocol approach focuses on the protocol flowing between the client and server interfaces as the common element.

Another important aspect of these approaches is that they are building blocks. In other words, they are not pure architecture types. In fact, the actual architecture adopted by an enterprise will usually be some combination of these approaches. And that is when it becomes more interesting!

A word of warning: No approach or architecture can completely solve problems caused by connectivity among federated databases. Regardless of the standards, interfaces, protocols, and so forth, there will always be some problems with retargeting a specific client application to a different server type. The challenge is to anticipate the problems relevant to your environment and seek the proper architecture to alleviate them.

For instance, consider the following difficult problem with retargeting applications—the collating sequences used by various database engines. When ORDER-BY or GROUP-BY clauses are used in a SELECT statement, the database engine sorts the result set on the specified columns. But, what is the sequence of this sorting when it involves character data? Character data from IBM DB2/MVS will be sorted in EBCDIC sequence, while character data from any UNIX database will be sorted in ASCII sequence. Further, what about multinational character sets? Realize that the German character set in Germany is sorted differently than the German character set in Belgium! And what if character sets are allowed to be mixed in the same column? It will be many years before DBMS vendors will provide flexible and efficient collating sequences based on international standards.

In the next sections, let's explore each of these approaches in more detail, remembering that combinations among the approaches have more practical value and that there are limitations to any of these approaches.

COMMON-INTERFACE APPROACH

A *common-interface* approach uses the interface (either client or server) as the common element in providing open connectivity. The principle is that the client application programs to one interface specification regardless of the current (or future) server types. That interface assumes the responsibility of transparency from the client to the server. That is, it is transparent to the client if and when the client is retargeted to another server type. The code of the client application does not change. And, hopefully the application works as intended!

As shown in Figure 10.5, the common interface consists of two components:

- generic interface (which the application utilizes)
- driver (which contains specific knowledge of a server)

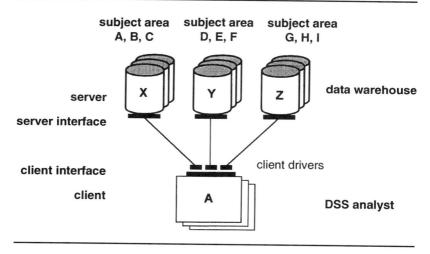

Figure 10.5.   Common interface.

The *generic interface* is the API to which the client application programs. It also resides on the client platform. The
vendor for the generic interface may or may not be the same
as the vendor for the server. In most situations, the vendor
is independent of a specific server vendor and achieves value
in supporting a variety of servers. On the other hand, the
driver is a complex code that takes the requests from and
results to the generic interface and processes them upon a
specific server. The driver contains knowledge of the capabilities (and quirks) of that specific server.

Over the last three years, there have emerged several
examples of products adopting the common-interface approach. An example of a common-interface product is Microsoft Open Database Connectivity (ODBC). The Microsoft
ODBC supports a common-interface approach, introduced
at a developers' conference in March 1992. Using the dy-

namic link library (DLL) mechanism in Windows, the appropriate ODBC driver is loaded when needed to connect to the proper data resource.

COMMON-GATEWAY APPROACH

A *common-gateway* approach utilizes a *database gateway* or simply gateway as the common element to alleviate differences among the target server types. The distinction with the common-gateway approach is that the server interface of one type is married with the client interface of another type via the gateway. This marriage extends the two-level client/server architecture into multilevel architectures.

In Figure 10.6, client A is written to the client interface

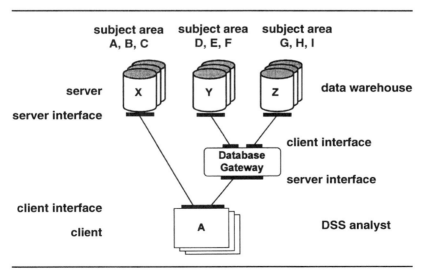

Figure 10.6.   Common gateway.

of server type X. By connecting to the database gateway as if it were a server of type X, client A now has access to database types Y and Z. The server interface of the gateway receives the requests from clients (as if it were a server of type X). The gateway then maps those requests into the proper format for another server type and uses the client interface for that server to resubmit the requests. The opposite mapping occurs to return the results to the client.

The gateway usually operates on a platform separate from the client or server platforms because of its role of mapping many clients to many servers. However, a gateway often resides on the same platform as a server when the gateway is mainly supporting or complementing that one server. Furthermore, there is technically no reason why a gateway cannot reside on the client platform, although the economics and administration issues do not justify this.

The effectiveness of the common-gateway approach is dependent upon the value added by the gateway component. When transforming requests for server X into requests for server Y, there are areas in which value could be added by the gateway:

- SQL syntax transformation from Type X to Type Y
- detection of semantic differences between X and Y
- conversion of data types
- generic system catalog access
- maintenance of transaction boundaries
- conversion of status code and messages
- mapping user identification and security checks
- load balancing and limits to server
- providing manageable control points for large networks
- mapping LAN transports to WAN transports; and so forth.

In addition, the gateway component could add value in nonconventional areas, such as:

- stimulating stored procedures against the database
- invoking stored procedures against nondatabase resources
- interfacing to/from messaging and mail facilities
- transferring bulk data directly between servers
- staging data to workgroup databases
- packaging data for better consumption by users

The common-gateway approach often complements and extends the other approaches. When used with some combination of common-interface and common-protocol, the common-gateway building block often adds flexibility to the system architecture. Because a database gateway operates on a platform that is usually inexpensive and separate from the client and server platforms, losses in efficiency are usually minimal.

An example of a common-gateway product is the Database Gateway for DB2 from Micro Decisionware, Inc. (MDI), now part of Sybase. It was developed as a joint project between Micro Decisionware and Microsoft, using the Microsoft Open Data Services. It accepts requests from client applications that use the SQL Server DB-Library or Microsoft ODBC client interfaces, translating the SQL syntax, data types, and so forth, appropriately. In addition, MDI supports other mainframe data resources (such as ADABAS, IMS, VSAM, IDMS) and simulates stored procedures under CICS to DB2 and other CICS/MVS data resources. MDI also pioneered the transfer function for staging data to and from the LAN database servers.

COMMON-PROTOCOL APPROACH

A *common-protocol* approach utilizes a well-defined open protocol to connect client applications to various server types.

Figure 10.7 shows each client interface accepting re-

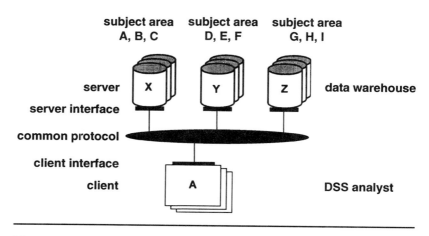

Figure 10.7. Common protocol.

quests from the client applications and translates those requests into the proper common protocol. Likewise, each server interface listens to the common protocol for requests, processes them, and translates the results into the proper common protocol for the clients. As discussed earlier in this chapter, a protocol is simply a stream of bits flowing between the client and server interfaces in both directions. It consists of the following:

- transport
- request commands and result responses
- data encoding and status codes
- SQL dialect (or specialization)

The main benefit of a common-protocol approach is that, as long as client and server interfaces generate or consume the same protocol, new client types or new server types can be added in the future without knowledge of the previous ones. The converse of this benefit is that the protocol must be robust enough to handle the diversity of functionality in current and future server types. Examples of products that use the common-protocol approach are:

- IBM Distributed Relational Database Architecture (DRDA)
- ISO Remote Database Access (RDA)

The IBM DRDA protocol is part of the SAA distributed database strategy to interconnect the IBM database servers (e.g., DB2/MVS, SQL/DS, SQL/400, DB2/2) and also facilitate the data delivery for IBM Information Warehouse framework. The transport for DRDA is SNA LU6.2 with the extension of including TCP/IP with IBM AnyNet. The intent of DRDA is to support fully distributed databases; however, the initial level of DRDA only supports a remote unit of work. With the release of DB2 2.3 (for an MVS client) and OS/2 DDCS/2 (for an OS/2 client), the first examples of a client interface that generate a common protocol have appeared.

The ISO RDA protocol is an emerging ISO international standard seeking universal data access. The transport for RDA is the ISO Open Systems Interconnect (OSI), with consideration by the SQL Access Group to extend the transport to TCP/IP. RDA only supports a remote unit of work with dynamic SQL, although an SQL statement can be prepared once and executed repeatedly.

COMBINATIONS AMONG THE THREE APPROACHES

Now that we have described the three approaches, let's examine an interesting combination of these approaches. Consider the combination of common-interface and common-gateway approaches, as shown in Figure 10.8. The applications have one client driver that connects into a database gateway. The gateway is then responsible for translating and routing the requests among several servers. The advantage is that the client drivers do not have to be distributed and managed on possibly thousands of workstations. Instead, a smaller number of gateways can consolidate the drivers and provide a simpler architecture to manage from the enterprise perspective.

With any of these combinations, a key issue is whether the common-interface specification allows the application logic to be aware of the type or capabilities of the server.

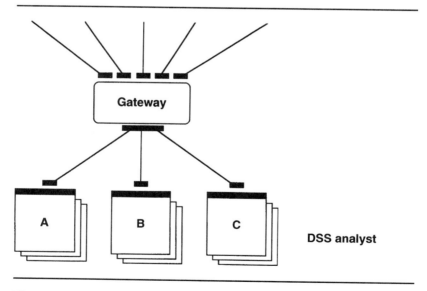

Figure 10.8.   Combining common interface with common gateway.

This is referred to as being *server-aware* or *capability-aware*, respectively, by the client application.

If neither is the case, the application logic will be independent of the server type or server capability; hence, retargeting should be easily accomplished. However, this implies that the application logic assumes a *least-common-denominator* characterization of the server. In other words, the application logic assumes a minimal set of characteristics that is the intersection of all current (and future) server types.

If *server-aware*, the application logic will contain a conditional code that is dependent on the server. For example, the application logic could detect through the generic interface that the server is Oracle version 6.12 under OS/2. The application could then generate SQL statements and use data types supported by this server type. Retargeting to other servers will be possible only if the application logic has anticipated those server types. Evolution to future server types is limited to those that are similar to current server types.

If *capability-aware*, the application logic will contain a conditional code that is dependent on specific capabilities of the server. For example, the application logic could detect whether the server can support an outer join, rather than whether the server is Oracle. This is more desirable than being server-aware since retargeting to a new server can be accomplished by properly profiling the server capabilities. However, the limitation is that someone must be smart enough to specify the appropriate capabilities in the beginning. One reason for new and enhanced servers is that they have new capabilities. These capabilities were probably not anticipated when the interface specifications were released. In the comparison section later, we will discuss the tradeoffs in design decisions with permissive interfaces (i.e., interfaces that allow server or capability awareness).

CLIENT/SERVER NETWORKING

The most confusing area within client/server architecture is figuring out: What connects to what, and how? Put simply, we have a *plumbing* problem of ensuring that DSS applications on client platforms can flow requests to important data warehouses on server platforms, and, receive the flow of (correct) results back!

This problem is very important for many corporations. Having invested huge sums in opening up mainframe, minis, and LAN database servers, these corporations are faced with establishing connectivity architectures and policies for workstation access to the various database servers. Because the

Figure 10.9. The plumbing problem of client/server networking.

desktop tools are exploding in variety and complexity, the connectivity requirements are changing constantly. In addition, the reliability of a connection from a specific client application to a specific database server is dependent on many factors and on many vendors.

The basic problem is that certain kinds of things are confused with other kinds of things. It is like comparing apples with oranges, or more like comparing plastic pipes with copper pipes; in any case, let's see if we can unscramble this confusion.

We need to consider the following different categories:

- development tools (custom and generic) for DSS applications
- client interfaces on client platform
- local-area transports (both logical and physical)
- wide-area transports (both logical and physical)
- server interfaces for data warehouses on server platform

Note that these categories fit together in a certain sequence, as shown in Figure 10.10.

On the left side, we first start with the DSS analyst using either a custom development environment or a generic tool, depending on what our application requirements are. In either case, a client interface is required to accept the client SQL request and process it against a database server. The usual function of this interface is to retrieve a relational result set and return it to the application. All of this resides on a specific client platform.

On the right side, we have the data warehouse on a server platform that is connected through some communication network. Here we have a number of options depending on which database servers are required. Also, with several platforms it is important to specify the telecommunication

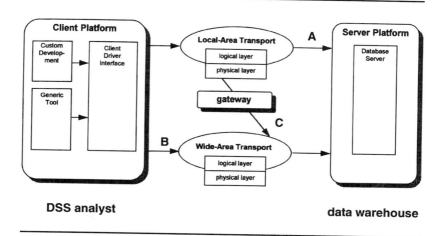

Figure 10.10. Client/server networking.

monitor that is controlling our connection. For example, there are significant differences in connecting to DB2 via TSO or via CICS.

In the middle is the tricky part. First, we need to consider the differences in local-area networks (LAN) versus wide-area networks (WAN). The architectures and protocols for LAN and WAN evolved from very different perspectives. Until recently, there was poor compatibility between the two types of networks. In every corporation with more than one site, there is some combination of LAN and WAN, in place, to be used for our client/server networking.

As shown in Figure 10.10, we can connect a client application to a database server via one of three routes:

A. *local-area network directly to the server platform.* The database server is then called a local server.

B. *wide-area network directly to the server platform.* In this case, we have a workstation that is not attached to a LAN but does have a WAN connection to the server platform. The database server is then called a *remote server*.
C. *local-area network to a wide-area network and then to the server platform.* In this case, the workstation is attached to a LAN that provides the WAN connection.

What are the tradeoffs among the three routes? Route A seems the simplest, and Route C seems the more complex.

LAN transports do provide higher bandwidth and reliability than WAN transports because of the inherent design constraints of using long-distance telecommunications lines. Moving data across the LAN can be 10 to 100 times faster and more reliable than across the WAN. Hence, the protocols for connecting applications to databases can provide a closer coupling between the two. Scrolling cursors across a vista of GUI-ish list boxes is difficult and inefficient with a 9600-baud switched SDLC line.

Historically, Route B is the oldest, stemming from the VT100-like asynchronous terminals, to 3270 synch terminal via bisynch lines, and then to coax-attached PC via SNA LU2. Even today, Route B is the largest installed base in most corporations. However, Route A is rapidly gaining ground with the percentage of LAN-attached PCs increasing daily. Further, Route C is the IBM-suggested way, with SNA forming the corporate backbone to interconnect the token-ring LANS via TIC-attachments on cluster controllers.

What is the best route? The trend is away from remote servers (as defined above) and toward local servers because of the requirements of greater bandwidth to the desktop. However, in most corporations, the issues of integrating with legacy systems and deploying enterprisewide applications weaken the argument for the one-big-happy-LAN design.

Route C is being adopted as the compromise architecture for consolidating resources on the LAN and for providing the only point of connect into the WAN. For consolidation and manageability, Route C is preferred by many corporations despite its greater complexity.

ENTERPRISE DATABASE CONNECTIVITY

In this chapter, we have examined so far the problems and approaches to open database connectivity for a DSS analyst accessing a data warehouse. This section discusses a framework for a corporation to analyze and determine an architecture for its database connectivity requirements. This framework is called *Enterprise Database Connectivity* (EDC) to highlight the problems of federated databases for data warehouses across the entire enterprise.

To deal with the complexity of the enterprise environment, EDC can be considered as having various layers of increasing functionality, consisting of the following:

- access management
- copy management
- warehouse management
- systems management

As illustrated in Figure 10.11, the higher layers build upon the required functions of the lower layers. These layers constitute the range of functions necessary to support the connectivity of databases across the enterprise, both for decision support and for operational systems.

Access management is managing the architecture to provide access from any client to any data resource. In particular, it focuses on the ability of a client application to directly access a local or remote database. Initially data access was focused on providing production applications access to the

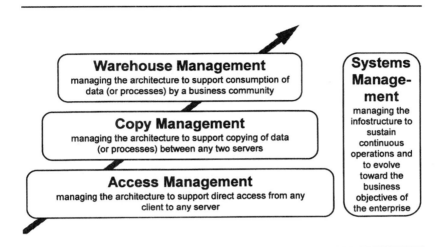

Figure 10.11.   The EDC layers.

local database. As we have discussed, data access has shifted to providing the DSS analyst access to various remote data warehouses using client/server architectures. With current technology, access management emphasizes solutions to the problems of database connectivity and client/server network plumbing.

Copy management is managing the architecture to provide coordination between any two data resources via the copying of data and processes. In particular, it focuses on the execution, scheduling, and monitoring of copies from one database to another for the purposes of data staging. With current technology, copy management deals with the distinction between extracts and replicas, refreshing volatile data, resynchronizing replicas, and copy recovery.

Warehouse management is managing the architecture to transform data (and processes) as it flows among data resources and to best deploy that data for its intended usage. In particular, it focuses on both direct and staged access by end users based upon an enterprise information directory. Warehouse management is more than a separate relational database that aggregates data from production databases. The challenge is to anticipate the usage patterns and to add value to the information through a variety of transformations.

Systems management is managing the infostructure to sustain continuous operations and to evolve toward the business objectives of the enterprise. The major barrier to widespread usage of client/server technology is the inability to manage the system across the enterprise. Systems management covers a wide range of functions, such as job scheduling, database backup, database recovery, problem determination, performance monitoring, data distribution, software deployment, security administration, user support, user training, application development, capacity analysis, change management, data administration, system strategies, and infostructure policy.

Another way to view these three EDC layers is as a triangle, as shown in Figure 10.12.

In the lower left is the personal desktop workstation with its local database (using Paradox or Access, for example). Access management is the architecture for connecting the desktop to enterprise data, realizing that this data is often stored in heterogeneous databases. The enterprise data is some combination of operationals, ODS, and warehouse data, as previously discussed. The staging of this data to and from workgroup databases on LAN servers is the focus of copy management. Warehouse management is concerned with the delivery of workgroup data (both operational and informational) to the desktop.

Finally, systems management ties it all together into a coherent framework with stable operations.

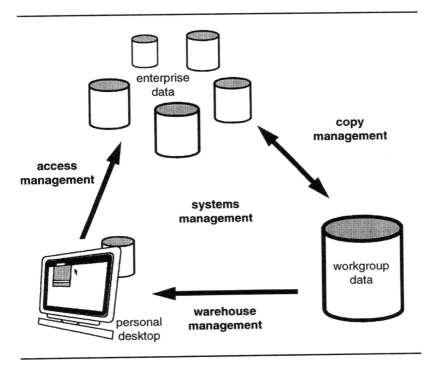

Figure 10.12.   The EDC triangle.

SUMMARY

The DSS analyst connects to the data warehouse using some variance of client/server architecture. This architecture separates the role of the client (i.e., DSS analyst) from that of the server (i.e., data warehouse) on separate platforms interconnected with specific interaction. This interaction consists of: a client interface, protocol, and server interface. The objectives of choosing the right interfaces and protocols are the portability of moving a DSS application or data warehouse to a new platform and the interoperability between platforms.

The use of proprietary architecture from a single vendor limits a company to support federated databases on heterogeneous platforms. The problems of retargeting a DSS application to a new data warehouse involve serious problems of SQL syntax, system catalog tables, collating sequences, and so forth. This chapter suggests that three approaches to open database connectivity are common interface, common gateway, and common protocol. The combinations among these approaches are the practical architectures used in many client/server systems. A key issue in developing DSS applications is whether the application is server-aware or capability-aware.

The confusing area of client/server networking is described as a plumbing problem between the client platform of the DSS analyst and the server platform of the data warehouse. Three routes for interconnecting client and server platforms are LAN only, WAN only, and LAN-to-WAN.

Finally, the larger context of Enterprise Database Connectivity is explained in terms of these functional layers: access management, copy management, warehouse management, and systems management.

References

Durrel, W., *Data Administration: A Practical Guide to Successful Data Management*, McGraw-Hill, New York, 1985.

Hackathorn, R.D., *Enterprise Database Connectivity*, John Wiley and Sons, New York, 1993.

IBM Distributed Data Library, *Distributed Remote Data Architecture,* IBM Publication SC26-4651, August 1990.

IBM System Application Architecture, *Common Programming Interface, Database Level 2 Reference,* IBM Publication SC26-4798, April 1991.

Information Processing Systems, Open Systems Interconnection, *Remote Database Access, Part 2: SQL Specialization Protocol,* ISO JTC1/SC21/WG3 N996, February 28, 1990.

Information Processing Systems, Open Systems Interconnection, *Remote Database Access, Part 1: Generic Model, Service and Protocol,* ISO JTC1/SC21/WG3 N995, March 24, 1990.

Inmon, W.H., *Building the Data Warehouse*, QED, 1990.

Inmon, W.H., *Data Architecture: The Information Paradigm*, QED, 1988.

Inmon, W.H., *Developing Client/Server Applications*, QED, 1993.

Inmon, W.H., *Third Wave Processing: DSS Processing on Database Machines*, QED, 1991.

Inmon, W.H., *Using DB2 to Build Decision Support Systems*, QED, 1990.

Inmon, W.H., *Using Oracle to Build Decision Support Systems*, QED, 1990.

Inmon, W.H., Kelley, C., *Rdb/VMS Developing the Data Warehouse*, QED, 1993.

Love, Bruce, *Enterprise Information Technologies: Designing the Competitive Company*, Van Nostrand Reinhold, New York, 1993.

Micro Decisionware, *Database Gateway Reference and Installation Guide*, Document Number 501-G01211-20, 1993.

Microsoft, *Microsoft Open Database Connectivity Software Development Programmer's Guide*, Version 2.0. Microsoft, 1993.

Narayan, Rom, *Data Dictionary: Implementation and Maintenance*, Prentice Hall, Englewood Cliffs, N.J., 1988.

Ross, R., *Data Dictionaries and Data Administration: Concepts and Practices for Data Resource Management*, McGraw-Hill, New York, 1984.

Welch, J.D., "Providing Customized Decision Support Capabilities: Defining Architectures," Auerbach Publishers, Penn Station, New York, 1990.

Welch, J.D., "Providing Customized Decision Support Capabilities: Implementation and Evaluation," Auerbach Publishers, Penn Station, New York, 1990.

Wertz, C., *The Data Dictionary: Concepts and Uses*, QED, 1987.

ARTICLES OF INTEREST

"Providing customized decision support capabilities: Defining architecture," Auerbach Publications, 1990, by J. D. Welch—decision support systems and architecture (based on the PacTel Cellular DSS architecture).

"A Case study: Implementing and operating an atomic data base," *Data Resource Management Journal*, Auerbach Publications, April 1992, by Dan Wahl and Duane Hufford; a description of the U.S. ARMY DSS data architecture.

"The need for reporting," *Data Base Programming/Design*, July 1992, by W. H. Inmon; the various kinds of reports found throughout the different parts of the architecture.

"Building the data bridge," *Data Base Programming/Design*, April 1992, by W. H. Inmon; ten critical success factors in building the data warehouse.

"Data warehouse—A perspective of data over time," *370/390 Data*

Base Management, February 1992, by W. H. Inmon; a description of the relationship of data warehouse and the management of data over time.

"Data structures in the information warehouse," *Enterprise Systems Journal*, January 1992, by W. H. Inmon; a description of the common data structures found in the data warehouse.

"Winds of change," *Data Base Programming/Design*, January 1992, by W. H. Inmon; data administration and the data warehouse— a description of how data administration evolved to where it is today.

"The cabinet effect," *Data Base Programming/Design*, May 1991, by W. H. Inmon; a description of why the data warehouse– centered architecture does not degenerate into the spider web environment.

"Going against the grain," *Data Base Programming/Design*, July 1990, by W. H. Inmon; a description of the granularity issue and how it relates to the data warehouse.

"At the heart of the matter," *Data Base Programming/Design*, July 1988, by W. H. Inmon; primitive and derived data and what the differences are.

"Neat little packages," *Data Base Programming/Design*, August 1992, by W. H. Inmon; a description of how data relationships are treated in the data warehouse.

"Metadata: A checkered past, a bright future," *370/390 Data Base Management*, July 1992, by W. H. Inmon; a conversation about metadata and how it relates to data warehouse.

"Guidelines for defining requirements for decision support systems," *Data Resource Management Journal*, October 1991, Auerbach Publications, by Paula Goldberg, Robert Lambert, and Katherine Powell; a good description of how to define end-user requirements before building the data warehouse.

"EIS and the data warehouse," *Data Base Programming/Design*, November 1992, by W. H. Inmon; the relationship between EIS and data warehouse.

"Chargeback in the information warehouse," *Data Management Review*, March 1993; chargeback in the data warehouse can be both a blessing and a curse—this article addresses the both sides of the issues.

"Now which is data, which is information," *Data Base Programming/Design*, May 1993; the difference between data and information.

"Data administration support for business process improvement," Duane Hufford, AMS; DW and DA. 1992, private circulation.

"A conceptual model for documenting data synchronization requirements," Duane Hufford, AMS; data synchronization and DW. 1992, private circulation.

"The unified data architecture: A systems integration solution," 1992, Auerbach Publications, by W. H. Inmon and Michael Loper; the original paper (republished in a revised state) suggesting that a data architecture was in order for future systems development.

"An architecture for a business and information system," *IBM Systems Journal*, Vol. 17, No. 1, 1988; a description of IBM's understanding of the data warehouse.

"Data patterns say the darndest things," *Computerworld*, Feb. 3, 1992, by W. H. Inmon and Sue Osterfelt; a description of the usage of the data warehouse in the DSS community and how informational processing can be derived from a warehouse.

"Information management for competitive advantage," *Strategic Systems Journal*, ACR, June 1993, by Jon Geiger; a discussion of how the data warehouse and the Zachman framework have advanced the state of the art.

"Information preservation," *CIO Magazine*, July 1993, by Jim Ashbrook; an executive's view of the data warehouse.

"An information architecture for the global manufacturing enterprise," 1993, by Robt Sloan, Hal Green, Auerbach Publications; a description of information architecture in the large-scale manufacturing environment.

"Retail technology charges up at KMart," by *Discount Store News*, Feb. 17, 1992; a description of the technology employed by KMart for their warehouse, ODS environment.

"Smoking out the elusive smoker," by Walecia Konrad, *BusinessWeek*, March 16, 1992; a description of database marketing in the advertising-restricted marketing environment.

PRISM SOLUTIONS TECH TOPICS

TIME DEPENDENT DATA STRUCTURES—This is a discussion of the different types of data structures and their advantages and disadvantages.

CREATING THE DATA WAREHOUSE DATA MODEL FROM THE CORPORATE DATA MODEL—These are the steps you need to take to create the data warehouse data model from the corporate data model.

REPRESENTING DATA RELATIONSHIPS IN THE DATA WAREHOUSE: ARTIFACTS OF DATA—These are the design issues for the building of data relationships in the data warehouse.

SNAPSHOTS OF DATA IN THE WAREHOUSE—This provides a description of the different types of snapshots and the advantages and disadvantages of each.

DEFINING THE SYSTEM OF RECORD—These are the design considerations of identifying and defining the system of record.

WHAT IS A DATA WAREHOUSE?—This Tech Topic defines what a data warehouse is and what its structure looks like. This is a basic discussion appropriate to anyone investigating the world of data warehouse.

CAPACITY PLANNING FOR THE DATA WAREHOUSE—This Tech Topic discusses the issue of capacity planning and projection for both disk storage and processor resources for the data warehouse environment.

OPERATIONAL AND DSS PROCESSING FROM A SINGLE DATA BASE: SEPARATING FACT AND FICTION—An early notion was that a single database should serve as the basis for both operational processing and DSS analytical processing. This Tech Topic explores the issues and describes why data warehouse is the appropriate foundation for DSS informational processing.

PARALLEL PROCESSING IN THE DATA WAREHOUSE—The management of volumes of data is the first and major challenge facing the data architect. Parallel technology offers the possibility of managing much data.

METADATA IN THE DATA WAREHOUSE—Metadata is an important component of the data warehouse. This Tech Topic discusses why, and what the different components of metadata are for the data warehouse.

LOADING THE DATA WAREHOUSE—At first glance, loading data into the data warehouse seems to be an easy task. It is not. This discussion is on the many different considerations of loading data from the operational environment into the data warehouse.

ACCESSING DATA WAREHOUSE DATA FROM THE OPERATIONAL ENVIRONMENT—Most flow of data is from the operational environment to the data warehouse environment, but not all. This Tech Topic discusses the "backward" flow of data.

INFORMATION ARCHITECTURE FOR THE NINETIES: LEGACY SYSTEMS, OPERATIONAL DATA STORES, DATA WAREHOUSES—This describes the role of operational data stores and the architecture that results when you mix an operational data store and a data warehouse.

INFORMATION ENGINEERING AND THE DATA WAREHOUSE—The data warehouse architecture is extremely compatible with the design and modeling practices of information engineering.

EIS AND DATA WAREHOUSE—EIS under a foundation of legacy systems is very shaky, but EIS under a data warehouse foundation is very solid, as detailed in this Tech Topic.

CLIENT/SERVER AND DATA WAREHOUSE—Client/server processing is quite able to support data warehouse processing. This Tech Topic addresses the issues of architecture and design.

DATA WAREHOUSE AND COST JUSTIFICATION—A priori cost justification is a difficult thing to do for a data warehouse. This topic discusses the issues.

REENGINEERING AND THE DATA WAREHOUSE—Many organizations are not aware of the very strong and very positive relationship between reengineering and the data warehouse. This topic identifies the relationship and discusses the ramifications.

THE OPERATIONAL DATA STORE—The operational counterpoint of the data warehouse is the operational data store (ODS). The ODS is defined and described in detail in this tech topic.

SECURITY IN THE DATA WAREHOUSE—Security takes on a very different dimension in the data warehouse than in other data processing environment. This Tech Topic describes the issues.

USING THE GENERIC DATA MODEL—Some corporations have a data model as a point of departure for the design of their data warehouse; others do not. The generic data model "jump starts" the data warehouse design and development effort.

SERVICE LEVEL AGREEMENTS IN THE DATA WAREHOUSE ENVIRONMENT—One of the cornerstones of online operations is the service level agreement. Service level agreements are applicable to the data warehouse but are implemented quite differently.

GETTING STARTED—The data warehouse is built iteratively. This Tech Topic describes in a detailed manner the first steps you need to take.

CHANGED DATA CAPTURE—The resources required for repeatedly scanning the operational environment for the purpose of refreshing the data warehouse can be enormous. This briefing addresses an alternative way to accomplish the same thing.

TELLING THE DIFFERENCE BETWEEN OPERATIONAL AND DSS—In every shop the issue arises—what is operational and what is DSS? This Tech Topic tells you how to distinguish between the two environments.

Index